Expository Writing:
50 Step-by-Step Lesson Plans with Formative Assessment
Designed for all students in a Differentiated Classroom

By Mary H. Crane, Ed. D.

Grades 4 - 8

A TO Z ™
BRANE
Educational
Consultants
www.braneconsulting.com

A Common Sense Approach to Effective Writing Instruction

ABOUT THE AUTHOR

Mary H. Crane has a diverse background that extends from business communications to education. Having served as a writing specialist, an instructional lead teacher, Title 1 coordinator, and academic specialist, she appreciates both the teaching and academic sides of education. While in the classroom, she developed writing techniques that resulted in 100% of her at-risk students to achieve proficiency on the state mandated writing test. Her passion for teaching writing to an ethnically-diverse student population inspired her to write this book.

Cover and graphic design by Byrd Graphics, Inc., Rochester, NY 14612

Copyright ©2011 by Mary H. Crane

Published by BRANE Publishing Co.

All rights reserved. No part of this book may be reproduced or transmitted in any form or by any means, electronic or mechanical, including photocopying, without permission in writing from the Publisher. Inquiries may be addressed to:
BRANE Publishing Co. | 3555 Raney Road | Titusville, FL 32780

Printed in the United States of America

ISBN 978-0-9828338-0-3

In memory of my loving stepson Larry who
took my pages and created a book that I am so proud to
present to all of you who love the art of writing.

Without his artistic talents and continuous creative energy,
this book would never have been published.
Someone once said that dedication is
not what others expect of you,
but what you can give to others.

Thank you, Larry,
for your inspiration and dedication
to believe in my cause
that every child can learn to write.

CONTENTS

CONTENTS

INTRODUCTION

Students across the nation continue to struggle in developing into good writers. This book is ideal for teachers who are looking for an easy and logical way to teach writing in the elementary and middle school grades especially for at-risk students who have such limited background knowledge. Each lesson is designed to teach writing in executable steps that produce a high student success rate. Through the use of the direct instruction model, each lesson plan follows a five-step process: skill introduction, modeling, guided practice, structured practice, and independent practice.

Most of the lesson plans are included with examples to make teacher preparation as painless as possible. Following the 50 carefully designed and explicit lesson plans are a wealth of resources including a template for the Writer's Notebook, front and back covers, Night Writes™ journal entries, "Word of the Day" entries as well as additional expository writing prompts. The only other materials needed are a 3-ring binder, an inexpensive black and white composition book, and a paperback dictionary for each student.

It has been proven that formative assessment is critical and dramatically improves students' writing. The strategies introduced in this book will help teachers to monitor, diagnose, and provide feedback to the students. By the completion of this book, students will be able to read and interpret a prompt independently, to organize their thoughts and plan their writing, and to write a detailed and thorough response.

Standard: The student uses writing processes effectively.

Objective: The student prepares for writing by recording thoughts, focusing on a main idea, grouping related ideas, and identifying the purpose for writing.

Skill Introduction: Discuss the importance of writing and how it is such an essential part of your education. Discuss how writers write for so many things: books, magazines, comic books, TV scripts, jokes, movies, crossword puzzles, maps, menus, newspapers, etc. Discuss how parents and professionals use writing everyday: moms write grocery lists, parents pay bills, doctors write prescriptions, police officers write tickets, etc.

Modeling: Think out loud with your students! Explain that you will be teaching them about the writing process. But, before you begin, let them know a little about yourself. On the overhead, list five things about yourself. Read them aloud. Next, write a paragraph about these five items. See list and biography sample on page 8.

Structured Practice: Tell students to list five items about themselves. After students have completed this task, ask them to share with the class. If students need help, coach them by asking questions like, "Do you have pets? How many brothers and sisters do you have? What is your favorite sport?"

Guided Practice: Have students take their five items and write a short paragraph about themselves. Keep your sample visible. It's okay if students use your paragraph as a reference point! It's day one and they need encouragement! Walk around the room and guide as needed. Comment on positive statements as well offering solutions to sentence writing.

Independent Practice: Upon completion of this exercise, students will begin completing "Who am I?" See sample statements on page 9.

It's All About Me!

1. writing teacher

2. five children and ten grandchildren

3. Snoopy collection

4. love to dance

5. read cookbooks

It's All About Me!

I have been the writing teacher at ABC Elementary School for five years. When I am not teaching school, I enjoy visiting with my five children and ten grandchildren. My favorite activities are Latin American dancing, reading cookbooks, and trying out new recipes on my husband. Another passion of mine is my tremendously large collection of Snoopys!

1. The most important thing I own is a _____

2. The best book I ever read was _____

3. My favorite game to play is _____

   because _____

4. When I am not at school, my favorite thing to do is _____

   because _____

5. What I like best at school is _____

   because _____

6. What really makes me happy is _____

   _____

   _____

7. My parents like for me to _____

   because _____

8. When I am with my friends, we like to _____

   because _____

   _____

9. I am so much different from my classmates because _____

   _____

10. I remember the most fun I had was when _____

    _____

    _____

    _____

DAY 2

Standard: The student uses writing processes effectively.

Objective: The student prepares for writing by recording thoughts, focusing on a main idea, grouping related ideas, and identifying the purpose for writing.

Skill Introduction: The class will complete "Who Am I?" Upon completion of answering the questions, students will take this information and write a paper about themselves.

Modeling: *Think aloud with your students!* Complete the survey and share responses. Next, share your completed essay with the class. Point out how you will take the ten questions and turn it into an essay. Demonstrate that it is a step-by-step process. See sample of completed "Who am I" followed by a sample essay.

Structured Practice: Ask students for ideas on how to complete "Who Am I?" Pick out several questions. For example, asking what their favorite thing to do after school is one they can all share ideas. Encourage students to tell why it is their favorite activity. Ask each student to explain their reasons why it is their favorite activity.

Guided Practice: Allow ample time for students to complete "Who Am I?" Walk around the classroom aiding students with completion of the questionnaire. Orally share some of the student responses with the rest of the class.

Independent Practice: Based on their responses, have students write a short essay about themselves titled, "Who Am I?"

Remember – this is Day 2! Do not allow students to become frustrated. Keep your essay visible. It's okay if students follow your writing pattern.

1. The most important thing I own is _my cookbook collection._

2. The best book I ever read was _Gone With the Wind._

3. My favorite game to play is _tennis_

   because _It's great exercise and I can also have some friendly competition with my girlfriends._

4. When I am not at school, my favorite thing to do is _try out new recipes_

   because _cooking is my best way to relax._

5. What I like best at school is _the students I teach._

   because _they have so much to offer and keep me young._

6. What really makes me happy is _when my students really seem to get what I'm teaching._
   In other words, the light goes on!

7. My parents would like for me to _complete my education_

   because _they know it is a goal that I want to achieve._

8. When I am with my friends, we like to _listen to music and go out to eat_

   because _it is a great way to learn about each other._

9. I am so much different from my classmates because _I have lived all over the world and been_
   to so many foreign counties.

10. I remember the most fun I had was when _I went to Disney World with two of my_
    grandchildren during Christmas. The Cinderella castle was spectacular!!!

Who Am I?

When I am not teaching students to write, my most favorite thing to do is try out new recipes on my family. It's my way to relax after a grueling day at school. With a collection of more than 200 cookbooks, my husband never knows what to expect for dinner. It may be Chinese stir-fry, Mexican fajitas, German goulash, or just a plain American hamburger and french fries.

I have to say that one thing that makes me so happy is when my students really seem to understand how to write an expository and narrative essay. In other words, when their lights go on, my body just can't control itself and I end up doing the "happy dance." The greatest reward for me is to watch students progress from hardly being able to write a paragraph to completing a full blown essay. I learn so much from my students as well. Besides that, they keep me on my toes and keep me young at heart.

There is a lot more to know about me. For example, my favorite sport to play is tennis. It is great exercise and a wonderful way to meet new people. At the end of a practice or match, we all meet at a restaurant and share stories about ourselves. It really doesn't get any better than that. Well, that's just a little about me. How about telling me about you?

Standard: The student uses writing processes effectively.

Objective: The student prepares for writing by recording thoughts, focusing on a main idea, grouping related ideas, and identifying the purpose for writing.

Skill Introduction: Introduce the Writer's Notebook. Explain that each student will receive a 3-ring notebook. There will be five sections labeled, "Word of the Day, "Scoring", "Notes", "Practice Work", and "Tests". Each section will be explained in detail when the section is introduced.

Modeling: *Think aloud with your students!* Show students the front and back cover sheet for the binder. The front sheet will have the student's name and classroom teacher's name. The back sheet will be all about the student. Place your paragraph, "All About Me" on the overhead. Tell students you are going to change the title, "All About Me" with "All About the Writer." Show your example. See sample of front and back covers in Appendix A.

Structured Practice: Ask four students their definition of a writer. Write down all of their ideas on the overhead. Look up the definition of writer and record it on the overhead. Have students copy the definition and place as the first entry in the section titled, "Word of the Day". Have students write a sentence using the word writer. Call on four students to read their sentences to the class.

Guided Practice: Have students complete the front sheet (Writer and Classroom Teacher's Name) and back sheet (All About the Writer) by copying over yesterday's assignment, "All About Me." Walk around the room and help students as needed. Have students draw a self portrait!

Independent Practice: When students have completed the two sheets, have them write down questions that they wanted to ask the teacher but never had the chance in the past two days. Tell students you will write them a personal note answering these questions.

DAY 4

Standard: The student uses writing processes effectively.

Objective: The student prepares for writing by recording thoughts and grouping related ideas.

Review: Read five or six student essays titled, "Who Am I?" Ask students if they can identify the student. In addition, comment on parts of essays that demonstrate the beginning steps of great writing.

Skill Introduction: Discuss letter writing and the various kinds of letters. Show an example of a business letter, friendly letter, thank you letter, congratulations, and condolences.

Modeling: ***Think aloud with your students!*** Point out the various parts of a letter: heading, salutation, body, closing, and signature. Discuss the difference between a business letter and personal letter. Explain the differences by showing students samples of these two types of letters.

Structured Practice: Place various letters on the overhead and have students identify what type of letter: business or personal. Call on students to identify what kind of letter: congratulations (anniversary, birthday, wedding, and graduation), condolences (death, illness, loss of home), thank you (dinner, personal favor, and hospitality), friendship note, complaint letter, letter to the editor, or a commendation letter (students, employees, and teachers). Point out the various parts of the letter in these samples.

Guided Practice: Have students identify types of letters and parts of a letter. Circulate the classroom to check for understanding. This is the step to see if students are grasping the skill. If 8 out of 10 students understand, move on to independent practice. If not, reteach the skill.

Independent Practice: Have students write a thank you note for a gift they received. Before the student begins, list type of gifts they might receive.

Heading ⋯⋯⋯⋯▶ Street Address on one line
City, State, Zip Code
Date

Salutation ⋯⋯⋯⋯▶ Means "hello." All words are capitalized.
A comma or colon follows the salutation.

Body ⋯⋯⋯⋯▶ Contains the main text or message.
Each paragraph is indented.

Closing ⋯⋯⋯⋯▶ Means "good-bye". The first word begins with
a capital letter. A comma follows the closing.

Signature ⋯⋯⋯⋯▶ Tells who wrote the letter.

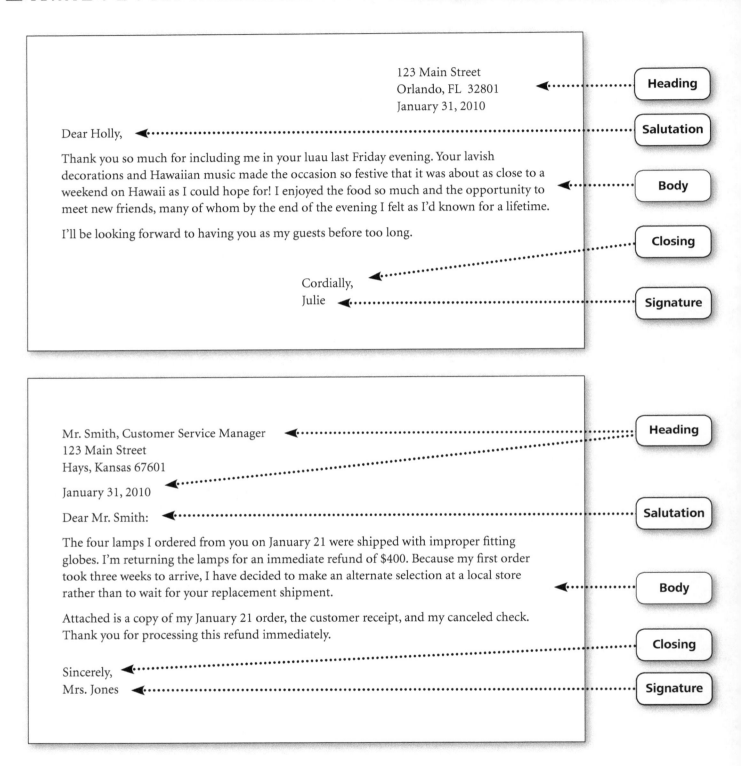

123 Main Street
Orlando, FL 32801 ◄·········· **Heading**
January 31, 2010

Dear Holly, ◄·········· **Salutation**

Thank you so much for including me in your luau last Friday evening. Your lavish decorations and Hawaiian music made the occasion so festive that it was about as close to a weekend on Hawaii as I could hope for! I enjoyed the food so much and the opportunity to meet new friends, many of whom by the end of the evening I felt as I'd known for a lifetime. ◄·········· **Body**

I'll be looking forward to having you as my guests before too long.

·········· **Closing**

Cordially, ◄··········
Julie ◄·········· **Signature**

Mr. Smith, Customer Service Manager ◄·········· **Heading**
123 Main Street
Hays, Kansas 67601

January 31, 2010

Dear Mr. Smith: ◄·········· **Salutation**

The four lamps I ordered from you on January 21 were shipped with improper fitting globes. I'm returning the lamps for an immediate refund of $400. Because my first order took three weeks to arrive, I have decided to make an alternate selection at a local store rather than to wait for your replacement shipment. ◄·········· **Body**

Attached is a copy of my January 21 order, the customer receipt, and my canceled check. Thank you for processing this refund immediately.

·········· **Closing**

Sincerely, ◄··········
Mrs. Jones ◄·········· **Signature**

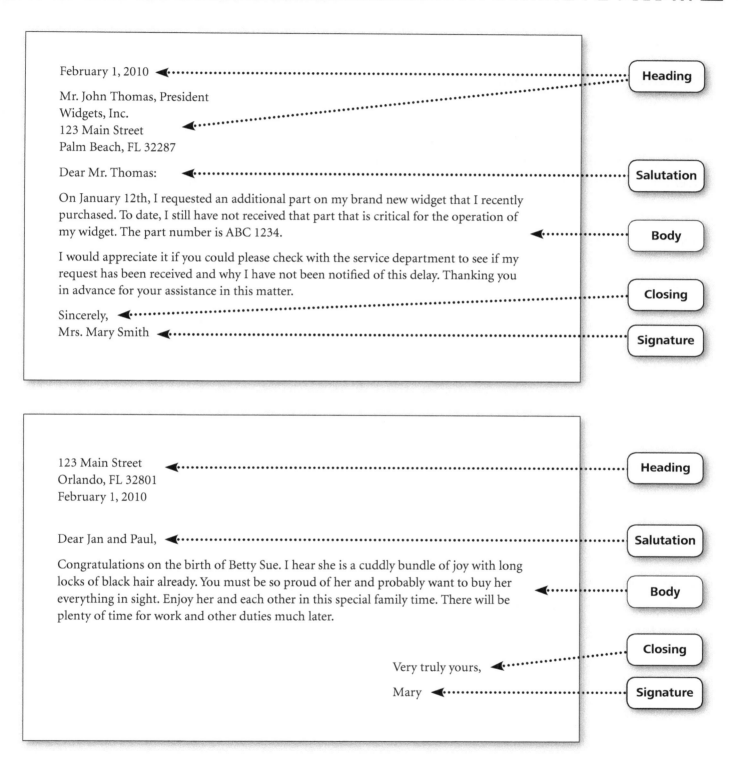

February 1, 2010 — **Heading**

Mr. John Thomas, President
Widgets, Inc.
123 Main Street
Palm Beach, FL 32287

Dear Mr. Thomas: — **Salutation**

On January 12th, I requested an additional part on my brand new widget that I recently purchased. To date, I still have not received that part that is critical for the operation of my widget. The part number is ABC 1234. — **Body**

I would appreciate it if you could please check with the service department to see if my request has been received and why I have not been notified of this delay. Thanking you in advance for your assistance in this matter. — **Closing**

Sincerely,
Mrs. Mary Smith — **Signature**

123 Main Street
Orlando, FL 32801
February 1, 2010 — **Heading**

Dear Jan and Paul, — **Salutation**

Congratulations on the birth of Betty Sue. I hear she is a cuddly bundle of joy with long locks of black hair already. You must be so proud of her and probably want to buy her everything in sight. Enjoy her and each other in this special family time. There will be plenty of time for work and other duties much later. — **Body**

Very truly yours, — **Closing**

Mary — **Signature**

DAY 5

Standard: The student uses writing processes effectively.

Objective: The student prepares for writing by recording thoughts, focusing on a main idea, and grouping related ideas.

Review: Select student thank you notes and place the selected letters on the overhead that demonstrate good letter writing. Comment on parts of their letters that show great promise of excelling in the writing process. Ask students to identify various parts of the letter and what they liked about the thank you notes.

Skill Introduction: Friendly letters are a gift from the heart. Even in the age of electronic mail, snail mail can strengthen friendship and family ties. They may become part of a journal or scrapbook.

Modeling: Explain to students that you are going to write a friendly letter to a family member. You will pick out three subjects that you will address in the letter. Model by making a graphic organizer (an outline) of the letter content. See attached samples.

Structured Practice: Have students plan their friendly letters. Ask students to write down whom they wish to write a letter. Pick several students and ask who and why they are writing the letter to this person. Have students copy your graphic organizer. Have them come up with three topics. Offer suggestions and have students share their topics.

Guided Practice: Have students list three details under each of the topics. Leave your sample on the overhead. Walk around the room and help students with details. Offer suggestions, praise students, and orally share some of their details with the class.

Independent Practice: Upon completion of their graphic organizer, have students write their letters. Show your sample on the overhead. It's okay if students copy some of your ideas. This is all new to them!

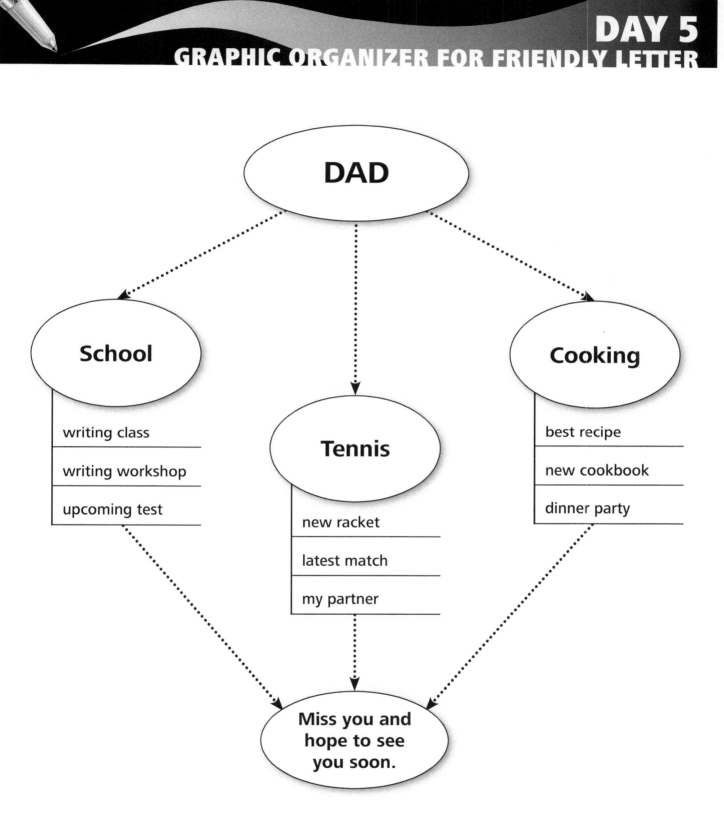

DAD

School

writing class

writing workshop

upcoming test

Tennis

new racket

latest match

my partner

Cooking

best recipe

new cookbook

dinner party

Miss you and hope to see you soon.

123 Main Street
Anywhere, FL 32780
January 31, 2010

Dear Dad,

I bet when you checked the address on the envelope, you couldn't believe it was me. It's been a long time since I've seen you and this time, instead of picking up the phone, I thought you just might like to receive a letter. After all, who doesn't like to receive mail!

First, let me tell you what is going on at school. My 8th grade students are just about to take the "BIG TEST" in a couple of weeks. I am putting the pedal to the medal and setting high expectations for all of them. They all can do it and they will. Those students who need some extra help have the option to attend an after school workshop. Believe it or not, more than half of my students stay after school to get that extra bit of instruction. Dad, I am so proud of them!

It's hard at times, but I'm still trying to keep active. Tennis is still high on my list of things to do. In fact, I just treated myself to a new tennis racket. It's about time, right? I was overdue for a new one, right? I'm justifying the cost of this beauty. It did prove me right, though, as I won my match last week. Of course, my partner Judy was on fire with her awesome serves.

You know when I'm not teaching writing or playing tennis, I'm cooking! And, you know how much I love to piddle in the kitchen. One of my dearest friends also knows how much I love to cook and bought me the latest best-selling cookbook on Mexican cuisine. Looking through the cookbook gave me some great ideas about our upcoming dinner party. I think I'll try a theme. How about Mexican? Brilliant idea, right?

Well, I need to start planning dinner. Perhaps I'll check my new cookbook for a chicken recipe. Wish you were here to help cut up the vegetables for me. Miss you and hope to see you soon.

Love,

Mary

Standard: The student uses writing processes effectively.

Objective: The student prepares for writing by recording thoughts, focusing on a main idea and grouping related ideas.

Review: Take a selection of student friendly letters and place on the overhead that demonstrate good letter writing. Comment on parts of their letters that show great promise of excelling in the writing process. Also ask students what makes these letters so special.

Skill Introduction: Friendly letters are written to friends and family. Business letters are written to someone you don't know. A business letter is more formal than a friendly letter, but can be just as fun to write. You can write to someone famous, like a singer or athlete, or to an owner of a business to express your ideas.

Modeling: Explain to students that you are going to write a business letter to someone you don't know. You will pick out 3 topics to address in the letter. Model a graphic organizer (an outline) of the letter content. See sample.

Structured Practice: Have students plan their business letter. Ask students to write down the person to whom they wish to write. Pick several students and ask who and why they chose this person. Next, have students check your graphic organizer and come up with 3 topics of their own. Offer suggestions and have students share their topics.

Guided Practice: Have students list 3 details under each topic. Leave sample graphic organizer on the overhead. Place the following sample questions on chart paper to stimulate the thought process. Walk around the room and help students with details. Offer suggestions, praise students, and share their details.

Independent Practice: After completing their graphic organizer, have students write their letters. Show your sample on the overhead. It's okay if students copy some of your ideas. Remember: Writing is a learned process.

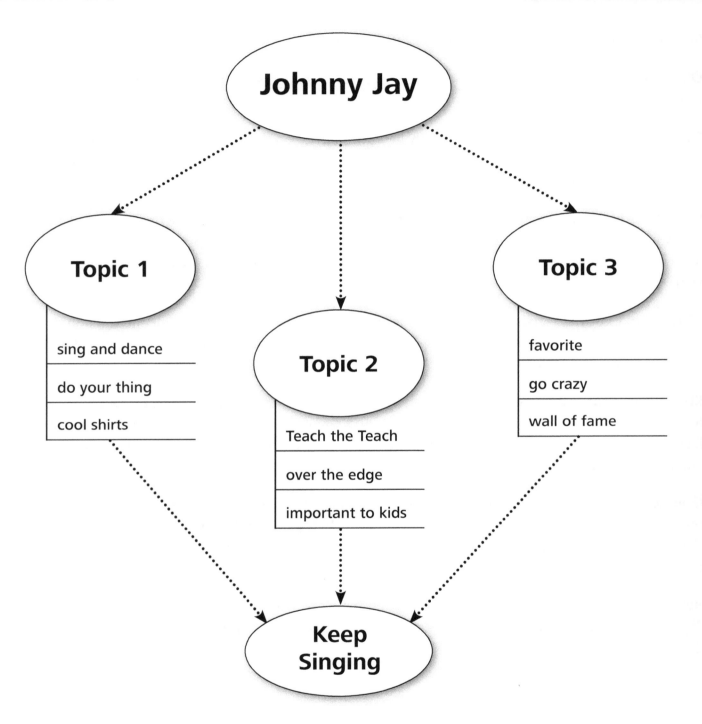

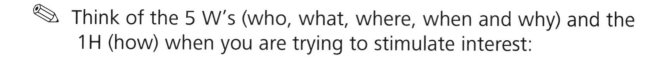

✎ Think of the 5 W's (who, what, where, when and why) and the 1H (how) when you are trying to stimulate interest:

✎ Who are some of the people who really think this person is great?

✎ What made you become interested in this person?

✎ What makes this person special?

✎ Where did this person begin his/her career?

✎ When did this person become famous?

✎ Why do you admire this person?

✎ Would you like to be like this person? Why?

✎ Why would you start a fan club for this person

✎ How long have you been a fan of this person?

123 Main Street
Anywhere, FL 33221
February 1, 2010

Dear Johnny Jay:

My name is Mary Smith and I am in the fourth grade at ABC Elementary School. Our class is learning how to write letters with our writing teacher, Dr. Crane. Right now we are writing letters to our favorite celebrities. I thought I would write to you because I am your number one fan.

I admire you for your great singing voice and your dancing ability. Those moves you put together in your last video titled, "Do Your Thing," were absolutely mind boggling. How do you sing and dance at the same time? Your breath control must be unbelievable. Where do you buy those really cool looking black and white shirts?

One of my most favorite songs is "Teach the Teach". That song is over the edge as far as the lyrics are concerned. It just makes me think of some of the crazy but caring teachers that help us learn at ABC Elementary. I hope you write more songs like "Teach the Teach". Another thing that I love about your songs is how you talk about what is important to kids. For instance, feeling like you are part of the group and knowing that you can make mistakes and not be put down is so real to me.

At ABC Elementary, we are collecting autographed pictures of our favorite celebrities. I would go absolutely crazy if you sent me one for our Wall of Fame. My biggest concern is making sure that I get to keep it. You know that you are the king of hip hop music and my friends would be so envious if I had your autographed picture.

I hope you keep singing songs and enjoy much more success.

Your fan,

Mary Smith

Standard: The student writes stories based upon personal reflections, observations, and experiences.

Objective: The student will write a journal entry for the first time.

Review: Pick out a selection of student business letters and place on the overhead that demonstrate good letter writing. Comment on parts of their letters that show great promise of excelling in the writing process. Ask students what makes these letters so special.

Skill Introduction: Journal writing means regularly writing down your thoughts and experiences. It is a learning tool based on the idea that students write to learn. When students write in journals, they can record such things as ideas and feelings, interesting things that have happened to them or information about interesting people. Journals offer students the opportunity to reflect on their world and expand their awareness of what is happening in their lives.

Modeling: Show students your composition book that will be used for your journal writing. Explain that this is an easy way to help improve writing skills. The more your write, the easier it becomes. Thinking aloud and commenting along the way, read your first journal entry to the students. See the attached sample.

Structured Practice: Give each student their own composition book for journal writing. The book will be called "Night Writes™." Explain to students that starting today, students will be expected to write at least a paragraph on a specific topic each evening. Explain to students that it is their responsibility to bring the composition book to class each day. At the beginning of each class period, explain that you will ask several students ke to share their entries. In order that students become familiar with the process, students will be allowed to complete their first journal entry in class. The first topic will be "Tell me about your family". Begin by having students orally share their initial thoughts about their family members. Prompt students to describe family members and expand on situations with their family and what makes them unique. Write their ideas and comments. Throughout the discussion, students may wish to write down some of their thoughts on a separate piece of paper. Allow ample time for students to become engaged in this process.

Guided Practice: Have students write at least one paragraph about their family. Circulate the classroom and offer suggestions, constructive remarks, questions, and encouragement whenever possible. Leave your sample visible for all students to see. Explain that this is free writing and a time to express feelings. Punctuation and spelling are not of prime concern. The writing will not be graded.

Independent Practice: The independent practice for Day 7 will be completed at home so as to allow students ample time to complete their first journal entry and be comfortable about the process. The "Night Writes™" entry for tonight will be "Who is your favorite teacher? Why? What do they do to inspire you?"

February 6, 2010

My Family

Sometimes I wonder how I was born into my family. It just seems that I am so far removed from them at times. Am I just different or are they just a bunch of weirdos?

I have a husband, two daughters and dog in my family. My husband is a sports nut! Not me! I can't stand to watch anything with a ball. That includes football, basketball, soccer, baseball, or whatever. He loves a big breakfast of eggs, bacon, toast, waffles, pancakes, and coffee. Me? I would rather just skip it altogether. One thing we do have in common, though, is we are both night owls.

My two daughters are as different as night and day. The older one named Sally just loves to watch college football, go to car races, play lots of tennis, and read sappy novels. She is really short, has blond hair, and dark brown eyes. Now Janie, the younger daughter, loves to play video games, text message all of her friends, read glamour magazines, and talk on the phone. She could care less about sports. In fact, the last time she played tennis, she never did hit the ball . . . not even once! She is quite tall, has auburn red hair, and hazel eyes.

My dog Snoopy has been a family member for ten years. He looks like the cartoon character and just happens to be a beagle. Just like the cartoon Snoopy, he is always running off and finding other people to pamper him. To say the least, he is spoiled rotten.

Well, that's just a brief overview of my family. They are a bit weird but I wouldn't trade them for anyone in the world!

Standard: The student will determine an audience and a purpose for writing.

Objective: The student will use resources to aid in the writing process.

Review: Ask for three students (Writers of the Day) to share their Night Writes™ journal entry with the class. This is not a graded assignment but check to see if each student has completed the homework assignment. ***Reward stickers for completion of "Night Writes™" has proven to be extremely effective.*** Write tonight's entry on the board. See list of selected topics in Appendix B.

Skill Introduction: Vocabulary is the building blocks of thought. It is the way we understand other people's ideas and express our own ideas. It is only logical then that people who know how to use words concisely and accurately find it easier to write. Introduce "Word of the Day". Explain to students that they will be given one word per day to place in the section titled, "Word of the Day" in their Writer's Notebook.

Modeling: Point out the section in their Writer's Notebook labeled "Word of the Day." Write the word of the day (writer) on the overhead. Demonstrate how you will look up the word and write the definition in your notebook. Next write a sentence using the word of the day in your notebook. See the attached sample. The "Word of the Day" list is located in Appendix C.

Structured Practice: ***For a writing class, it is critical that each student have their own dictionary.*** Have each student write their first entry in the section titled "Word of the Day". The first word of the day is writer. Have students write down your definition of the word. Call on several students to repeat the definition. Next, have students write a sentence using the "Word of the Day". Have several students read their sentence to the class. This is a daily exercise which should take about 5 minutes per day to complete. Today's first day session of this exercise is anticipated to take a lot longer!

Guided Practice: To ensure that students understand the "Word of the Day" process, have students find the second word of the day (elated) in their dictionary and write down the definition as their second entry in their section of the Writer's Notebook titled, "Word of the Day". After the student has written down their definition, have the student write at least two separate sentences using the word "elated". Circulate throughout the classroom to ensure all students are grasping this practice. Help students who are having trouble finding the word in the dictionary or writing two sentences using this word. As you circulate throughout the classroom, you may wish to orally share some of the sentences students have written.

Independent Practice: On a separate sheet of practice paper, have students write a paragraph (five to six sentences) on this topic: "Would you like to be a writer? Why or why not. Collect the papers. Review and share one of the student paragraphs with students on Day 9. Do not grade these papers. We are only eight days into being outstanding writers.

writer . . .

a person who is able to write and has written something

One of the most exciting things that will happen to me this year will be creating a new classroom of writers. Soon these students will be writing complete stories that will entertain and excite me. I can't wait.

Standard: The student will identify the purpose for writing and the audience for which it is intended.

Objective: The student will understand the difference between expository and narrative writing.

Review: Ask three students (Writers of the Day) to share their Night Writes™ journal entry with the class. Post Night Writes™ topic for homework. Remember: This is not a graded assignment but teacher should check and reward students for completion of their homework.

Word of the Day: Have students find the "Word of the Day" in the dictionary and write down the definition. Have students write a complete sentence using the word. Ask several students to read their sentences.

Skill Introduction: Introduce students to the two types of writing – expository and narrative. Expository is a type of writing that is used to explain, describe, give information, or inform. Narrative is story telling.

Modeling: Think aloud! Expository writing provides information, explains, clarifies or defines. Examples of expository writing include "how to" papers, comparing and contrast writing, providing information, business letters, research papers, personal reactions and subject writing. Narrative writing describes an experience, event, or sequence of events in the form of a story. Examples of narrative writing include writing that shares events from your own life, writing that shares thoughts on a specific topic, and writing that reflects your own personal experiences. Give topics of both types of writing. For example, how to make a cake would explain the process. This would be a piece of expository writing. However, if you wrote about the time you made a surprise birthday cake for your mom and how it turned out to be a disaster, that would be a piece of narrative writing. Give several more examples of these two types of writing.

Structured Practice: On the board, write the word "expository" at the top of the left column and the word "narrative" at the top of the right column. Ask students for words that define expository; ask students for words that define narrative. List them under the appropriate heading. Prompt students for responses if they are having trouble coming up with the appropriate definition. Next, write examples of types of both expository and narrative writing (See attached samples. The answers are included for your edification). Ask students if this is expository or narrative writing. Ensure that all students have had an opportunity to answer. ***This is a participatory exercise . . . students should not be writing!***

Guided Practice: Have students turn to the section of their notebook labeled "Notes". This will be the students' first entry for this section. Students will copy down your notes (See teacher notes sample). As you circulate throughout the classroom, check to ensure that students are writing down the definitions and are able to distinguish between the two types of writing.

Independent Practice: Following the completion of students taking notes and circulating the classroom for understanding, have students complete the attached worksheet on their own.

Is it Expository or Narrative?

Writing that reports new information that has been learned by checking the research (books, internet, magazines). ➤ *Expository*

Writing that shares an event or experience from your own life. ➤ *Narrative*

Writing that explains a step-by-step procedure of something. ➤ *Expository*

Writing that shares information about newsworthy people, places or events. ➤ *Expository*

Writing that shares events of the writer's life in his or her own words. ➤ *Narrative*

Writing that shows the similarities and differences of two subjects. ➤ *Expository*

Writing that communicates business-related material to people in the workplace. ➤ *Expository*

Writing that tells a story based on the writer's imagination. ➤ *Narrative*

Writing that provides your reaction to what you have read in a book, letter, poem, etc. ➤ *Expository*

Expository Writing - provides information, explains, clarifies, or defines

Types of expository writing:

- A "how to" paper

- Defines something

- Shows similarities and differences of two subjects

- Provides information clearly

- Communicates business-related material to people in the workplace

- Reports new information that has been learned by checking the research (internet, reference books, magazines, etc.)

- Shares information about newsworthy people, places or events

- Provides your reaction to what you have read in a book, letter, poem, etc.

Narrative Writing - describes an experience, event or sequence of events in the form of a story

Types of narrative writing:

- Shares an event or experience from your own life experience

- Tells a story based on the writer's imagination

- Shares events of the writer's life in his or her own words

1. **What are the two types of writing?**

    _____

    _____

2. **Is the writing expository or narrative?**
    Write an E for expository or an N for narrative.

    _____ Writing that communicates business letters to other people in the workplace.

    _____ Writing that provides a personal reaction to something you have read in a book.

    _____ Writing that provides information, explains, clarifies, or defines.

    _____ Writing that shares events of the writer's life in his or her own words.

    _____ Writing that reports new information that has been learned by checking the research (internet, reference books, magazines, etc.)

    _____ Writing that tells a story based on the writer's imagination

    _____ Writing that shows similarities and differences of two subjects

    _____ Writing that is a "how to" paper

Standard: The student will identify the purpose for writing and the audience for which it is intended.

Objective: The student will focus on learning the components of expository writing.

Review: Ask three students (Writers of the Day) to share their Night Writes™ journal entry with the class. Post Night Writes™ topic for homework. Remember: This is not a graded assignment but check and reward students for completion of the homework. Next, review the differences between expository and narrative writing – expository writing informs and narrative writing tells a story.

Word of the Day: Have students find the "Word of the Day" in the dictionary, copy the definition, and write a complete sentence using the word. Ask several students to read their sentences.

Skill Introduction: Explain what an expository writing prompt is, what it does, how to decipher a prompt, and how an expository piece of writing is put together.

Modeling: _Think out loud!_ Explain that prompts are the topic for the student's writing. Prompts have two basic parts: the writing topic and the directions for writing. Students need to read the prompt to figure out what the topic is all about. Explain that for an expository prompt or topic, students are to explain, inform, give steps, cite reasons, and show examples. The clue words for an expository prompt are tell why, tell how, or explain. Show samples of prompts to students (See attached teacher notes). Discuss the structure briefly. State that the students will soon be able to write a five paragraph essay which will include an introduction, three supporting paragraphs, and a conclusion. Emphasize to students that you will lead and guide them through every step of the way.

Structured Practice: _This is a participatory exercise . . . students should not be writing!_
On the board, place the attached page that describes an expository piece of writing. Randomly ask students what an expository prompt does. Students should respond with what is included in the overhead. Randomly ask students the clue words for an expository prompt. Call on at least five students to identify clue words. It's okay if they repeat the same words. Repetition leads to improved performance. Ensure that all students have had an opportunity to answer.

Guided Practice: Have students turn to the section of their notebook labeled "Notes". Students will copy down your specific notes titled "An Expository Prompt". Circulate throughout the classroom to ensure that students are on task and are following your notes. Emphasize that these notes are their road maps to successfully completing the assignment. Explain that their notes should look like your notes. Recognize students who are following your directions.

Independent Practice: After students have completed copying your notes, check for understanding. Next, have students copy down the six prompts in their notes. They are to circle the topic, draw a rectangle around the clue word(s) and underline what to write about.

Expository Prompt

What does it do? Explains

Informs

Instructs

Defines

Clarifies

Clue Words: Tell why

Tell how

Explain

Five Paragraphs: Introduction

First reason or step

Second reason or step

Third reason or step

Closing

Circle the topic, draw a rectangle around the clue word(s) and underline what to write about

Prompt 1:

Every season has advantages and disadvantages.

Before you begin to write, think which season you think is the best of all.

Now explain why you believe the season you chose is better than other seasons.

Prompt 2:

Many people like one kind of animal for a pet more than other animals.

Before you begin to write, think about what kind of animal you believe makes the best pet.

Now explain why you believe the animal you chose makes the best pet.

Prompt 3:

What do you know how to do well? Can you shoot a basketball or make cookies, for example?

Before you begin to write, think about something you do that you can teach

Then write a how-to essay.

Prompt 4:

Write an essay explaining how to get along with your teacher. Make sure younger friends reading it will know what to do.

Prompt 5:

The local newspaper is having a "Good Citizen" essay contest. Think about the characteristics a good citizen should have. Explain what a good citizen should be like.

Prompt 6:

We all have things we really enjoy doing outside. You may like to play ball, jump rope, or play with your pet.

Before you begin writing, think about things you really enjoy doing outside. Now explain to the reader of your paper, what you enjoy doing outside.

Standard: The student will use prewriting strategies to generate ideas and formulate a plan.

Objective: The student will focus on learning the components of expository writing.

Review: Ask three students to share their Night Writes™ journal entry with the class. Post Night Writes™ topic for homework. Next, review the definition of an expository writing prompt. Reiterate to students that when given an expository prompt, a student will be given a why, how or what question about the prompt.

Word of the Day: Have students find the "Word of the Day" in the dictionary, copy the definition, and write a complete sentence using the word. Ask several students to read their sentences.

Skill Introduction: Students will focus on expository writing. The teacher will explain what it does, how to decipher a prompt, and how an expository piece of writing is put together.

Modeling: *Think out loud!* Explain that expository writing must include reasons supported by details and examples. It usually consists of five paragraphs. Explain to students that the introduction will tell the reader what topic they are explaining followed by two or three reasons why they chose that topic. The next three paragraphs will focus on those reasons (a paragraph per reason). Emphasize that this is the area of writing where students need to provide details and examples to support their reasons. The final paragraph restates what they chose, the reasons behind their choice, and a concluding sentence. Stress to students that you will lead and guide them through every step of the way.

Structured Practice: This is a participatory exercise . . . students should not be writing!
On the board, write the following:

> **We all have things we really enjoy doing outside.**
>
> **You may like to play ball, jump rope, or play with your pet.**
>
> **Before you begin writing, think about things you really enjoy doing outside.**
>
> **Now explain to the reader what you enjoy doing outside.**

Read the prompt in its entirety. Have several students define the topic. Ask one student to come to the board and circle the topic. For the second procedure of deciphering the prompt, ask several students what they believe are the clue words. Have one student come to the board and draw a rectangle around the clue word(s). Last, ask students what they believe is what they will write about. Have one student underline the portion of the prompt that tells the student what to write about. Ask students for reasons why this prompt is expository. Now that the topic is identified, ask students what kinds of things they like to do outside. Make a list. There will be duplication in the answers. However, repetition leads to improved performance. Ensure all students have had a chance to answer.

Guided Practice: Have students turn to the section of their notebook labeled "Notes". Students will follow along with you and copy down your graphic organizer exactly as you have it on the board. (See attached). Circulate throughout the classroom to ensure that students are on task and are drawing the graphic organizer exactly like yours. Emphasize that these notes are their road maps to successfully completing the assignment.

Explain that their notes should look like your notes. Recognize students who are following your directions. Explain to students that this is a graphic organizer, or, for short, a G.O. Upon completion of the drawing, have students write in the center bubble, "Things I like to do outside." Next have students place three things they like to do outside in the next three bubbles. Emphasize to students that the graphic organizer is just a plan and just a method to organize their thoughts. Circulate throughout the classroom. Leave the list posted of possible things students like to do outside. At this point, have students put pencils down to discuss the details. Ask students why they like to do these specific things outside. Are these the reasons or the details? Have students think of reasons they like to do these activities. Stimulate thought by asking about something that happened to them when they did a certain activity. Have some students talk about the activity and why it is exciting? Explain to students that tomorrow they will be completing parts of their graphic organizer (G.O.) by filling in the details with a few words.

At this stage, there is no independent practice with the graphic organizer.

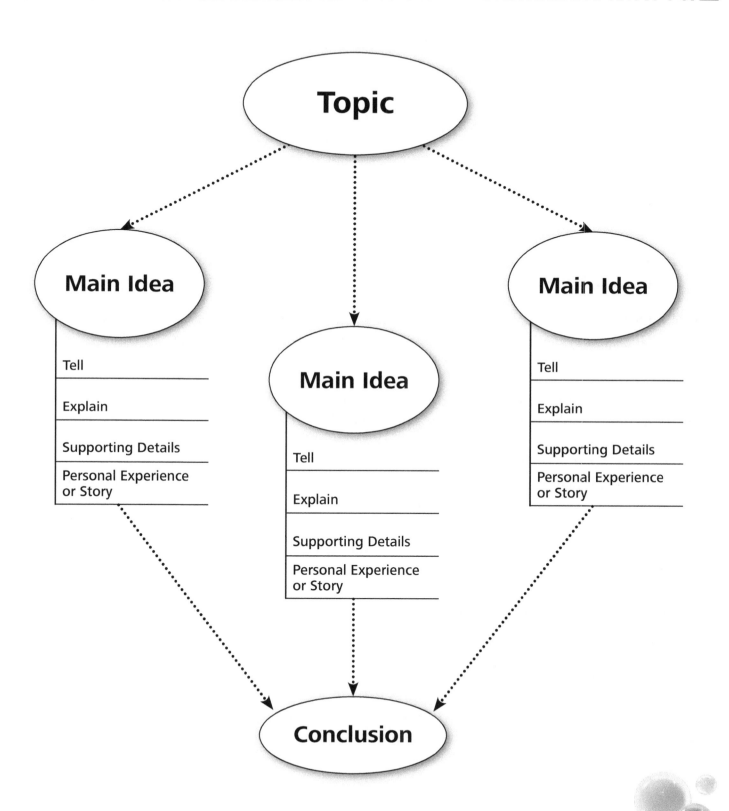

DAY 12

Standard: The student will use prewriting strategies to generate ideas and formulate a plan.

Objective: The student will focus on learning the components of a graphic organizer.

Review: Ask three students to share their Night Writes™ journal entry with the class. Post Night Writes™ topic for homework. Next, review the definition of an expository writing prompt. Ask students to name the clue words for expository by having them write them on a 3x5-inch card. After circulating throughout the classroom, have several students read their answers. Place Day 10 Sample on the overhead and review to ensure all students understand the clue words and parts of an expository essay.

Word of the Day: Have students find the "Word of the Day" in the dictionary, copy the definition, and write a complete sentence using the word. Ask several students to read their sentences.

Skill Introduction: Students will continue to focus on the graphic organizer for an expository piece of writing. Place sample of a graphic organizer from Day 11 on the board and explain the various parts again.

Modeling: *Think out loud!* Reread yesterday's prompt to the class. Place the prompt on the board so all students can follow along. (See next page). Underline the clue words that identify this to be an expository prompt. Next, place your empty graphic organizer on the overhead and describe how you will fill it out. Point to each section. Explain that the top large bubble is the topic and will include your introduction. The second set of three bubbles will be your three main ideas (reasons or steps). Each set of bubbles will support your main idea by telling about your main idea, explaining your main idea, supporting it with details, and supporting it with a story. This is the process to follow for each of the three main ideas. The bottom circle is your conclusion which sums up the topic and your three main ideas. Emphasize to students you will guide them through every step of the way.

Structured Practice: *This is a participatory exercise . . . students should not be writing!* Ask students to find their graphic organizers that they started yesterday. Have every student point to and state their topic. Then call on various students to state their main ideas. If students copy other student's ideas, it's okay. They are in the process of learning the steps. At this point, students should have at least filled in the topic and three main ideas or reasons. Now place a sample of your completed graphic organizer that shows the details of each main idea. Have students point out the details to you – telling, explaining, giving a supporting detail, or personal experience/story.

Guided Practice: Explain to students that this is a graphic organizer, or, for short, a G.O. Upon completion of the topic and three main ideas, have students write in their center bubble, "Things I like to do outside." Next have students place three things they like to do outside in the next three bubbles. Circulate throughout the classroom. Leave the list posted of possible things kids like to do outside. At this point, have students put pencils down to discuss the details. Ask students why they like to do these certain things outside. These are the reasons or the details. Have students think of why they like to do these certain activities outside. Fill in why they like to do these activities. They do not have to give complete sentences . . . just a few words why they like to do these activities outside. For the conclusion, summarize why you like these activities. Again, circulate throughout the classroom and help students with this portion of the graphic organizer.

At this stage, there is no independent practice with the graphic organizer.

Topic

- We all have things we really enjoy doing outside. You may like to play ball, jump rope, or play with your pet.

- Before you begin writing, think about things you really enjoy doing outside.

- Now explain to the reader what you enjoy doing outside.

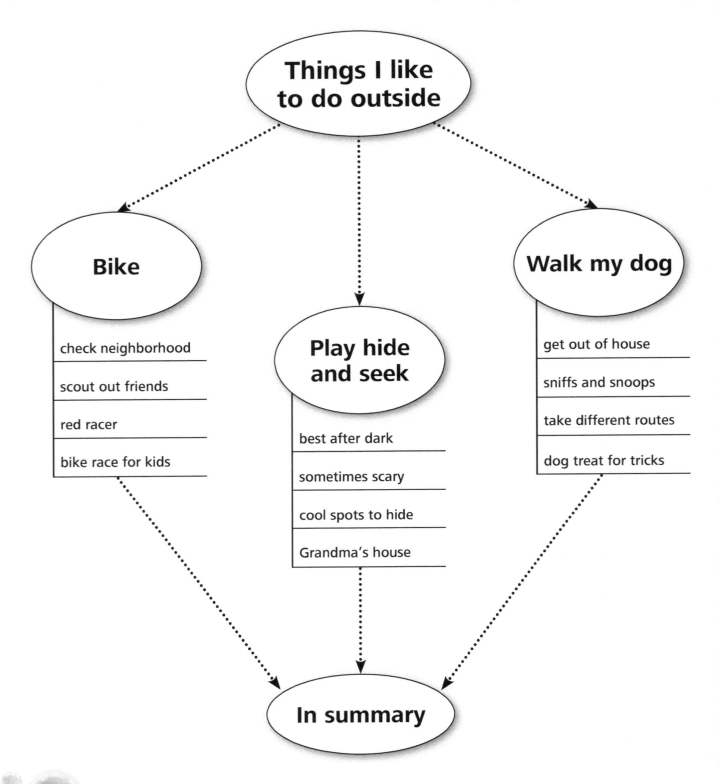

Things I like to do outside

Bike

check neighborhood

scout out friends

red racer

bike race for kids

Play hide and seek

best after dark

sometimes scary

cool spots to hide

Grandma's house

Walk my dog

get out of house

sniffs and snoops

take different routes

dog treat for tricks

In summary

Standard: The student will use prewriting strategies to generate ideas and formulate a plan.

Objective: The student will complete a graphic organizer.

Review: Ask three students to share their Night Writes™ journal entry with the class. Post Night Writes™ topic for homework. Next, review the parts of the Graphic Organizer, or "G.O". Use the sample from Day 11.

Word of the Day: Have students find the "Word of the Day" in the dictionary, copy the definition, and write a complete sentence using the word. Ask several students to read their sentences.

Skill Introduction: Students will continue to focus on the graphic organizer for an expository piece of writing.

Modeling: *Think out loud!* Place example of the completed graphic organizer from Day 11 on the overhead and explain the various parts again. The teacher will discuss the topic, three main ideas, the four parts that must be included in each main idea, and the conclusion.

Structured Practice: *This is a participatory exercise . . . students should not be writing!* Ask students to share their graphic organizers with the class. If students are intimidated about bringing their graphic organizers to the front of the class, have students verbally explain their graphic organizer.

Remember: This is the first time they have completed an outline (graphic organizer). Estimation is that about 50% will have it done. BE PATIENT!!

Guided Practice: Place the sample prompt on the overhead along with the blank organizer. Have students complete the graphic organizer. Circulate the room and encourage students with the process. As you are making your rounds, orally cite good examples of completed work to the rest of the class.

There is still no independent practice with the graphic organizer.

Everyone enjoys time with their family. What is the best day you have ever spent with your family?

Think about the best day that you ever spent with your family. Think about reasons that made it the best day ever.

Complete a graphic organizer that explains why this was the best day you ever spent with your family. Include at least three reasons that explain what made it the best day.

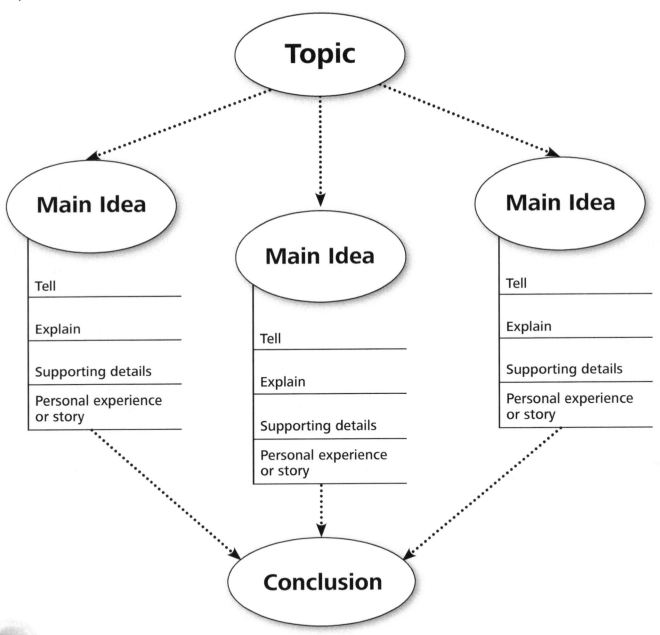

Everyone enjoys time with their family. What is the best day you have ever spent with your family?

Think about the best day that you ever spent with your family. Think about reasons that made it the best day ever.

Complete a graphic organizer that explains why this was the best day you ever spent with your family. Include at least three reasons that explain what made it the best day.

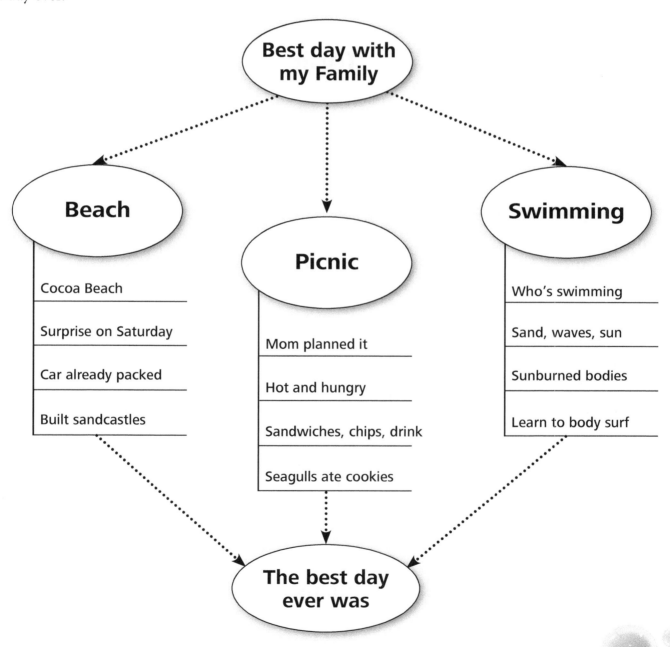

Best day with my Family

Beach

Cocoa Beach

Surprise on Saturday

Car already packed

Built sandcastles

Picnic

Mom planned it

Hot and hungry

Sandwiches, chips, drink

Seagulls ate cookies

Swimming

Who's swimming

Sand, waves, sun

Sunburned bodies

Learn to body surf

The best day ever was

Everyone has a favorite color.

Think about what yours is and why it is your favorite. Think about things that are your favorite color and how they make you feel.

Complete a graphic organizer explaining three reasons why _____ is your favorite color. Remember to use specific details to support and explain your reasons

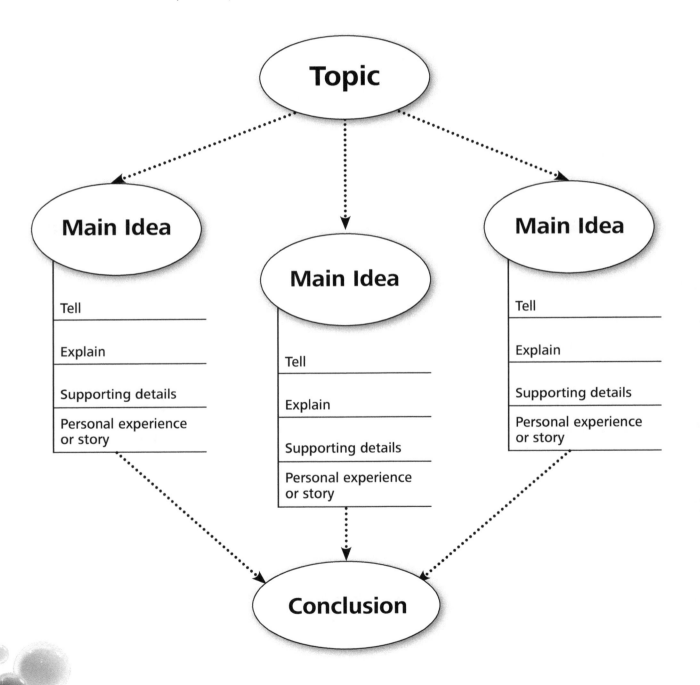

Everyone has a favorite color.

Think about what yours is and why it is your favorite. Think about things that are your favorite color and how they make you feel.

Complete a graphic organizer explaining three reasons why _____ is your favorite color. Remember to use specific details to support and explain your reasons

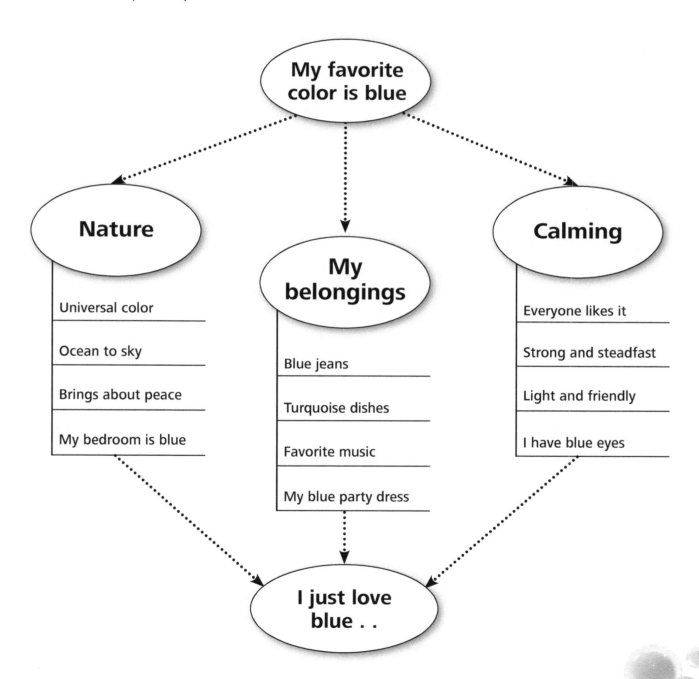

DAY 14

Standard: The student will use prewriting strategies to generate ideas and formulate a plan.

Objective: The student will complete a graphic organizer.

Review: Ask three students to share their Night Writes™ journal entry with the class. Post Night Writes™ topic for homework.

Word of the Day: Have students find the "Word of the Day" in the dictionary, copy the definition, and write a complete sentence using the word. Ask several students to read their sentences.

Skill Introduction: Students will continue to focus on the graphic organizer for an expository piece of writing.

Modeling: Think aloud! Place the sample of the completed graphic organizer from Day 13 on the overhead. Discuss the topic, three main ideas, the four parts that must be included in each main idea, and the conclusion. See sample attached.

Structured Practice: *This is a participatory exercise . . . students should not be writing!* Ask students to share their graphic organizers with the class. If students are intimidated about bringing their graphic organizers to the front of the class, have students verbally explain their graphic organizer.

Remember: This is only the second time they have completed an outline (graphic organizer). Estimation is that about 70% will have it completed. BE PATIENT!!

Guided Practice: Place the sample prompt on the overhead along with the blank organizer. Have students complete the graphic organizer. Circulate the classroom and encourage students with the process. As you are making your rounds, orally cite good examples of completed work to the rest of the class.

There is still no independent practice with the graphic organizer.

Rainy days bring out our emotions and can bring on many feelings and memories.

Think about what you do on rainy days. Do you enjoy rainy days or dislike them?

Complete a graphic organizer explaining three reasons why you like or dislike rainy days. Remember to use specific details to support and explain your reasons.

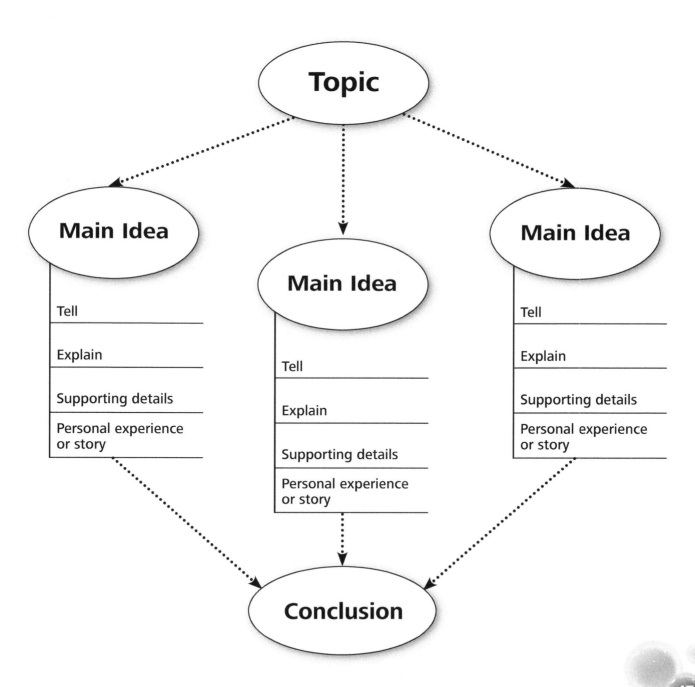

Rainy days bring out our emotions and can bring on many feelings and memories.

Think about what you do on rainy days. Do you enjoy rainy days or dislike them?

Complete a graphic organizer explaining three reasons why you like or dislike rainy days. Remember to use specific details to support and explain your reasons.

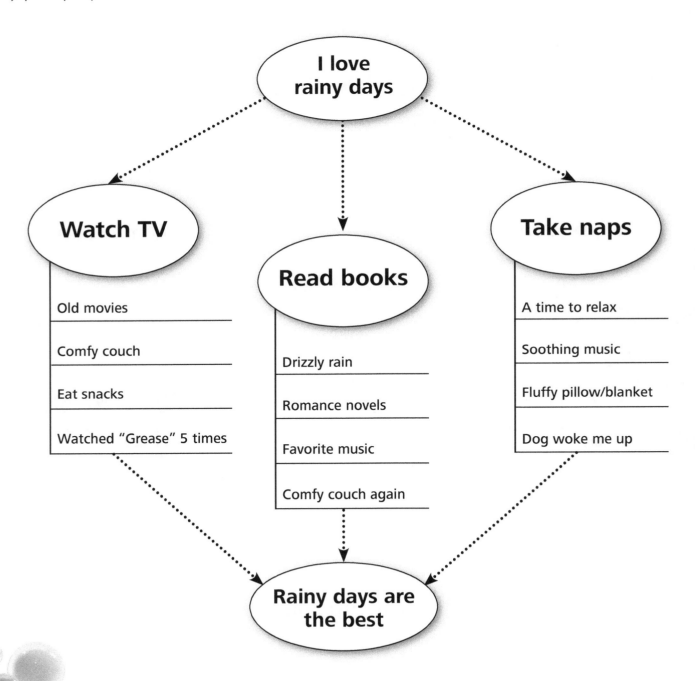

Standard: The student will use prewriting strategies to generate ideas and formulate a plan.

Objective: The student will complete a graphic organizer.

Review: Ask three students to share their Night Writes™ journal entry with the class. Post Night Writes™ topic for homework. Next, review the parts of the Graphic Organizer, or "G.O". Use the sample from Day 11.

Word of the Day: Have students find the "Word of the Day" in the dictionary, copy the definition, and write a complete sentence using the word. Ask several students to read their sentences.

Skill Introduction: Students will continue to focus on the graphic organizer for an expository piece of writing.

Modeling: *Think aloud!* Place the sample of the completed graphic organizer from Day 14 on the overhead and explain the various parts again. Discuss the topic, three main ideas, the four parts that must be included in each main idea, and the conclusion.

Structured Practice: *This is a participatory exercisev. . . students should not be writing!* Ask students to share their graphic organizers with the class. If students are intimidated about bringing their graphic organizers to the front of the class, have students verbally explain their graphic organizer.

This is the third time that students have completed an outline (graphic organizer). Approximately 85% of students should have the graphic organizer completed.

Independent Practice: Place the sample prompt on the overhead. The students have fifteen minutes to read the topic and complete the graphic organizer on their own. There will be no guided practice. Collect graphic organizers and check for mastery. If less than 85% of students have not completed, repeat days 13 and 14.

Topic

- Best friends are special people in our lives.

- Think about your best friend and reasons that you like him or her. Think about things that you enjoy doing together.

- Complete a **graphic organizer** telling about your best friend. Include three reasons why she or he is your best friend. Remember to use specific details to explain and support your reasons.

Standard: The student will write a draft appropriate to the topic, audience and purpose.

Objective: The student will begin writing an introduction based on the completed graphic organizer.

Night Writes: Ask three students to share their Night Writes™ journal entry with the class. Post Night Writes™ topic for homework.

Word of the Day: Have students find the "Word of the Day" in the dictionary, copy the definition, and write a complete sentence using the word. Ask several students to read their sentences.

Review: Have students draw the graphics (bubbles and lines) of a graphic organizer. Have one student come to the front and demonstrate how it is done and explain what is to be included in each section.

Skill Introduction: Discuss different ways that a student could begin an essay. Various methods are a question, quotation, a surprise, exclamation, personal opinion, sound, a fact, or statement.

These are Great Grabbers!

Modeling: Place the sample completed graphic organizer from Day 14 on the overhead and explain that it's time to write the introduction or opening paragraph. Point to the topic and say that there are various ways to begin. **Think out loud and write on the overhead!** *"Should I begin with a question, quotation, exclamation, personal opinion, sound, a fact, or a statement? So many ways to begin! I'll try three different ways.**

Question: *Do you like rainy days? I just love them. Why? These are the only days that I can watch TV when I want to, catch up on my reading, and have the luxury to take a nap.*

Quotation: *"Mom, I just heard that it is supposed to rain today. I've been waiting for a day like this forever. Finally! Now I'll have a chance to do what I want to do like watch TV, catch up on my reading, and take a long nap."*

Whodunit: *As I was creeping past my brother's bedroom, I heard this sound that startled me for a moment! What could it be? I dashed to the window and was in for my surprise of the day. It took me totally off guard. Rain was streaming down the window and splattering in the yard. I was delighted as now I could have the day to catch up on watching TV, reading my favorite books, and taking a nice long nap.*

Structured Practice: *This is a participatory exercise . . . students should not be writing!*
Return student's graphic organizer from day 15. Explain to students that they will only be using one of these three ways to write an introductory paragraph today (question, quotation, or whodunit). The prompt dealt with their best friend and three reasons why this person was their best friend. Have selected students share their best friend and reasons why her or she is their best friend. Orally make up introductions based on their reasons. Ask selected students if this Great Grabber used a question, quotation, or a whodunit.

Guided Practice: Have students turn to their "Notes" section in their Writer's Notebook and write "Introduction" at the top of the sheet. Have students copy down the nine different methods of beginning an expository essay. Next, have students place a check next to question, quotation, and whodunit. Tell students that they will write their opening paragraph by using one of the three methods (question, quotation, whodunit) discussed today. Circulate throughout the classroom and orally share student's opening paragraphs that are on target. This is also the time that you should be giving assistance to students who are struggling. Give them a chance and encourage them.

Nine great grabbers to begin your expository essay:

- Question
- Quotation
- Whodunit
- Exclamation
- Personal opinion
- Sound
- Fact
- Startling Statement
- Humorous Statement

Standard: The student will write a draft appropriate to the topic, audience and purpose.

Objective: The student will begin writing an introduction based on the completed graphic organizer.

Night Writes: Ask three students to share their Night Writes™ journal entry with the class. Post Night Writes™ topic for homework.

Word of the Day: Have students find the "Word of the Day" in the dictionary, copy the definition, and write a complete sentence using the word. Ask several students to read their sentences.

Review: Discuss the three different ways that a student could begin an essay - question, quotation, and a whodunit. Have students share their introductions. Ask students to identify whether the student began with a question, quotation, or a whodunit.

Skill Introduction: Discuss three new ways a student could begin an essay – exclamation, personal opinion, or a sound effect.

Modeling: Place the same teacher graphic organizer from Day 14 on the overhead. Model by writing the following three new types of introductions (Great Grabbers) with the same prompt.

> *Exclamation:* *Goodness gracious! What a whopper of a storm! I can't believe it's really raining so hard! I just love it when it rains like this. What a great opportunity for me to do all the things I love to do - watch TV, read books, and take naps.*

> *Personal Opinion:* *Rain is the most wonderful weather in the whole wide world. It makes you want to do things that you normally never have a chance to do like watch endless hours of TV, read books that have been sitting on your shelves for months, and taking those well-deserved naps.*

> *Sounds*: *Trickle, trickle, drip, drop, drip! I hear the rain hitting my bedroom window. The sounds are so soothing to me. It just makes me want to do all the things that I normally don't have time to do. Here's my chance to watch TV, read a good book, or take an afternoon nap.*

Structured Practice: ***This is a participatory exercise . . . students should not be writing!*** Have students use their graphic organizer from Day 15 (My best friend). Explain to students that they will only be using one of these three new Great Grabbers to write an introductory paragraph today (exclamation, personal opinion, or sounds). Reiterate that the prompt deals with their best friend and three reasons why this person is their best friend. Choose different students to share the name of their best friend and reasons why he or she is their best friend. Orally make up Great Grabbers based on their reasons. Ask selected students if this introduction used an exclamation, personal opinion, or sound.

Guided Practice: Instruct students turn to their "Notes" section in their Writer's Notebook and place a check next to exclamation, personal opinion, and sounds. Explain to students that they will write their opening paragraph by using one of these three different methods (exclamation, personal opinion, or sounds) discussed today. Circulate throughout the classroom and orally share student's opening paragraphs that are right on target. This is also the time that you should be giving assistance to students who are struggling. Give them a chance and frequently encourage them.

Standard: The student will write a draft appropriate to the topic, audience and purpose.

Objective: The student will begin writing an introduction based on the completed graphic organizer.

Night Writes: Ask three students to share their Night Writes™ journal entry with the class. Post Night Writes™ topic for homework.

Word of the Day: Have students find the "Word of the Day" in the dictionary, copy the definition, and write a complete sentence using the word. Ask several students to read their sentences.

Review: Discuss the three additional techniques that a student could begin an essay – exclamation, personal opinion, and sound effect. Have students share their introductions. Ask students to identify whether the student began with an exclamation, personal opinion, or sound effect.

Skill Introduction: Discuss the three final techniques a student could begin an essay – fact or two types of statement (humorous or startling).

Modeling: Place the same teacher graphic organizer from Day 14 on the overhead. Model by writing the following three new types of introductions with the same prompt.

> ***Fact:*** *Everyone knows that rain helps grass, plants and flowers grow. I just wish that it would help me grow too! Unfortunately, it doesn't but I still look forward to rainy days. It's an opportunity for me to do all the things I love to do- watch TV, read books, and take afternoon naps.*

> ***Statement (humorous)****: It's raining, it's pouring, and the old man is snoring. Why would an old man snore when it's raining? That's silly! Maybe it's because he likes to take naps when it rains. That's just one of the things I like to do when it rains. I also enjoying curling up on the couch and watching TV shows or reading a good book.*

> ***Statement (startling):*** *The umbrella was originally intended for shade from the hot Egyptian sun. I thought it was invented to protect us from the rain. Wrong again! It seems weird, but it's true! Rain doesn't bother me and personally I don't care if it rains all day. This is my chance to do all the indoor things I love – watch my favorite TV shows, read a romantic book, or just lay down and take a nice and peaceful afternoon nap.*

Structured Practice: *This is a participatory exercise . . . students should not be writing!*
Use the graphic organizer from Day 15 (My best friend). Explain to students that they will only be using one of these last three ways to write an introductory paragraph today (fact, silly statement, surprise sentence). Reiterate that the prompt dealt with their best friend and three reasons why this person was their best friend. Choose different students to share the name of their best friend noted on their graphic organizer and reasons why he or she is their best friend. Orally make up introductions based on their reasons. Ask selected students if this introduction used a fact, silly statement, or surprise sentence.

Guided Practice: Have students turn to their "Notes" section in their Writer's Notebook and place a check next to fact, silly statement and surprise sentence. Tell students that they will write their opening paragraph by using one of these three different methods (fact, humorous statement or startling statement) discussed today. Circulate throughout the classroom and orally share student's opening paragraphs that are on target. This is also the time that you should be giving assistance to students who are struggling. Give them a chance and encourage them.

Standard: The student will write a draft appropriate to the topic, audience and purpose.

Objective: The student will begin writing an introduction based on the completed graphic organizer.

Night Writes: Ask three students to share their Night Writes™ journal entry with the class. Post Night Writes™ topic for homework.

Word of the Day: Have students find the "Word of the Day" in the dictionary, copy the definition, and write a complete sentence using the word. Ask several students to read their sentences.

Review: Discuss the three final ways that a student could begin an essay –fact, silly statement, or a startling sentence. Have students share their introductions. Ask students to identify whether the student began with a startling statement.

Skill Introduction: Students will be able to create an interesting lead through one of the nine methods provided over the past three days.

Modeling: *Think out loud with students:* "Introductions can grab the reader's attention, let the reader know what you are going to talk about, show a plan for what you are going to be talking about, or state what the reader will learn in this essay." Review the nine techniques shown on Day 16 titled, "Great Grabbers".

Structured Practice: *This is a participatory exercise . . . students should not be writing!* Call on students to answer the following questions. This should be a give and take session. First, ask several students to name the nine techniques that they can use to begin an expository essay. Ensure that students can name at least four or five techniques to begin an expository essay. Next circulate throughout the classroom and call on students to name one of the nine ways to begin an expository essay. Make sure that all nine methods were named before moving on to the next step. Place the following prompt on the board.

Many people like one kind of animal for a pet more than other animals.

Before you begin to write, think about what kind of animal you believe makes the best pet.

Now explain why you believe the animal you chose makes the best pet.

A list of various openings will follow the sample on Day 19. Ask students which of the nine methods was used to begin the essay. Ask students what else is to be included in the opening paragraph (the three main ideas or three reasons).

Guided Practice: Pass out the attached worksheet for students to complete. It is the same type of exercise that was used for structured practice. This time, however, students are to try and complete this worksheet on their own. Circulate throughout the classroom and praise students who are completing the worksheet successfully. This is also the time that you should be giving assistance to students who are struggling. Give them a chance and encourage them. Upon completion, read answers and have students check their own work. Collect worksheets and review for student mastery.

Many people like one kind of animal for a pet more than other animals.
Before you begin to write, think about what kind of animal you believe makes the best pet.
Now explain why you believe the animal you chose makes the best pet.

1. Dogs are the best pets in the whole world. They are loyal and friaendly to their owners They are intelligent and make great companions. In addition, dogs make great playmates.

2. Which animal do you think makes the best pet? I think dogs make the best pets because they are loyal, intelligent and make great playmates.

3. Humans have made pets of animals for thousands of years. From something as common as a cat to something as exotic as a lion, history has shown that humans have kept such animals as pets. However, there is one animal that stands out above the rest. Time after time, dogs have proven themselves to be loyal, protective and loving companions. This is why they make the best pet to adopt.

4. Yippee, Skippie! My dream came true! I am so excited! Dad and mom finally let me have a pet dog. I've always wanted a dog because all my friends have them. It seems they make the best pets. They are loyal, protective and make great playmates.

5. Zipppity doo dah, zippity de yay. I can't wait til the end of the day. Plenty of sunshine comin my way. Here comes my pet dog, he's ready to play! This is just me being silly thinking about why dogs make such great pets. They are so loyal, intelligent, and make fantastic playmates.

6. Bow wow! Bow wow wow! That's a familiar sound from my pet dog. He's always there for me. That's why dogs make such good pets. They are loyal, protective and make fantastic playmates.

7. "Gosh, Dad, I hope that one day I can have a pet dog. I can't think of anything in the world I would like more than a dog for a pet." It seems that the thought of owning a pet dog has been going through my head forever. All my friends have dogs. They seem to be so loyal, loving, friendly, and never let you down.

8. One evening I was all by myself just watching an old TV comedy rerun. My hand was dangling down off the side of the couch. I felt this wet sensation touching my fingers. I peered down and there was my dog licking my palm. I can always count on him being right there. That's why dogs make the best pets. They are so loyal, loving, and make great companions.

Everyone has jobs or chores.

Before you begin writing, think about why you do one of your jobs or chores.

Now explain why you do one of your jobs or chores.

1. "I know your favorite TV show is on, but it's time for you to walk the dog," remarked Mom.

2. Woof! Woof! I hear Spot, my fluffy white poodle, sounding off his vocal chords. It must be time to walk him again.

3. Do you have a chore that you have to do every day? I do. Mine is walking my dog named Spot.

4. They say that dogs are man's best friend. I tend to agree. Otherwise, I wouldn't take over the job of walking Spot, my fluffy white poodle, every day.

5. There are four types of poodles: teacup, toy, miniature and standard. I happen to have the miniature kind of poodle. Mine seems to be pretty spunky especially when I have to walk him every day.

6. As I trudged into the kitchen, I heard this persistent scratching. It sounded as if it was coming from the pantry. I quietly tip toed to the pantry and placed my ear on the door. More scratching. The noise was nerve wracking but somewhat familiar. I should have known. It's Spot, my fluffy white poodle signaling that it's time for his walk.

7. Everyday! Even weekends! It never ends! Walking Spot, my fluffy poodle, is my job that I must handle.

8. Girls and boys just can't wait to do chores. NOT! This is the silliest remark that I've heard in a long time. The reasons we do chores is because we have certain responsibilities. Mine is walking my poodle named Spot.

DAY 20

Standard: The student will write a draft appropriate to the topic, audience and purpose.

Objective: The student will begin writing an introduction based on the completed graphic organizer.

Night Writes: Ask three students to share their Night Writes™ journal entry with the class. Post Night Writes™ topic for homework.

Word of the Day: Have students find the "Word of the Day" in the dictionary, copy the definition, and write a complete sentence using the word. Ask several students to read their sentences.

Review: Discuss the nine techniques that a student could begin an essay. Review previous notes and discuss in detail.

Skill Introduction: Students will be able to complete a graphic organizer and create an interesting lead through one of the nine techniques provided over the past three days. The prompt will be a guided practice exercise.

Guided Practice: Place the following prompt on the board. Have students copy down the prompt on a sheet of paper. Instructions are to first complete the graphic organizer and then write the opening paragraph using one of the nine methods discussed over the past four days. Circulate the classroom and extend help if necessary.

This is your time to encourage, praise and give support! Upon completion, collect papers for your review.

Teachers help us learn many things.

Before you begin writing, think of a teacher who has been special to you.

Explain why this teacher is special to you.

Standard: The student will write a draft appropriate to the topic, audience and purpose.

Objective: The student will learn how to use transition words in an expository essay.

Night Writes: Ask students to share their Night Writes™ journal entry with the class. Post Night Writes™ topic for homework.

Word of the Day: Have students find the "Word of the Day" in the dictionary, copy the definition, and write a complete sentence using the word. Ask several students to read their sentences.

Review: Discuss the nine ways that a student could begin an essay. Review worksheet examples from Day 19 (structured and guided practice examples). Ask students to identify which type of introduction was used.

Skill Introduction: Expository writing explains. It has five paragraphs, three main ideas (reasons) and uses transition words. Students will learn the definition of transition words and how they are used in expository writing.

Modeling: *Think aloud*. Transitions are phrases or words used to connect one idea to the next. Transitions are used to help the reader move from one idea to the next. They help link sentences and paragraphs together to make the essay sound better.

Structured Practice: Have students turn to their "Notes" section of the Writer's Notebook and write down the "Top Ten Transition Trios" listed on page 60. Explain that once they begin writing complete essays, they will be using these transition words. Each essay will use three transition words and they have been grouped together to help make them easier to remember. When students begin writing their second, third and fourth paragraphs, they will use transition words. Call on students to pronounce these words. Ensure they understand how they are to be used. Explain that additional transition words will be added as they are introduced.

Guided Practice: The class will not participate in guided practice today but will move on to an independent practice.

Independent Practice: Place the following prompt on the overhead. Have students copy down the prompt on a sheet of paper. Instructions are to first complete the graphic organizer and then write the opening paragraph using one of the nine methods discussed over the past four days. Students are also to pick out one group of transition words that they will use. Write the transition word outside each of the main ideas. Students may use their notes to select their three words. Upon completion, collect papers to check for mastery. This independent practice should not take more than 15 minutes to complete. Remember that students are working on timing as well. At the conclusion of this session, share what would be your ideal job along with your opening paragraph (see attached sample).

The Top Ten Transition Trios

first	at the start
second	soon after
third	in the end
once	at the beginning
next	then you are ready
last	after
to begin with	before
having done that	during
after completing	later
one reason that	initially
another reason that	the next step
the last reason that	finally
in the beginning	originally
as you move on	moreover
subsequently	as a result

Think of an ideal job for you when you grow up.

Before you begin writing, think of reasons why this would be a good job for you.

Write to explain why this is your ideal job.

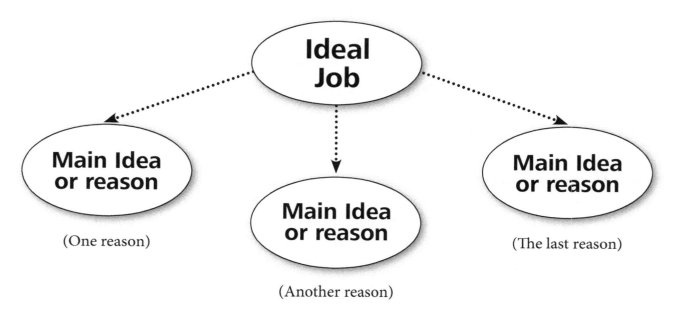

How do people decide what an ideal job would be? I have always known I wanted to be a teacher. I have many people who have influenced my life choices and many fond memories to validate I am making the right choices. To me, being a teacher is not only my ideal job, but it is a quality that is imprinted in my heart.

Standard: The student will write a draft appropriate to the topic, audience and purpose.

Objective: The student will learn how to write the second paragraph in an expository essay.

Night Writes: Ask 3 students to share their Night Writes™ journal entry with the class. Post "Night Writes™" topic for homework.

Word of the Day: Have students find the "Word of the Day" in the dictionary, copy the definition, and write a complete sentence using the word. Ask several students to read their sentences.

Review: Discuss transition words. Pull up the Day 21 sample and review the groups of transition words. Review that transitions are phrases or words used to connect one idea to the next. Transitions are used to help the reader move from one idea to the next. They help link to sentences and paragraphs to make the essay sound better.

Skill Introduction: Expository writing explains. The first paragraph (or introduction) has been completed. We have used a Great Grabber to begin our essay - a question, quotation, whodunit, exclamation, personal opinion, sound, fact, or startling statement or humorous statement. The essay has five paragraphs, three reasons (why, what, or how) and uses transition words.

Modeling: *Think aloud.* The topic is my ideal job. We all have expressed what we believe is our ideal job. To date, we have completed our G.O. (graphic organizer), our opening paragraph and come up with three transition words that will tie our other three paragraphs together. At this time, pick out several students papers that have been reviewed that have positive qualities. Share with the class what makes these papers special. It may be the graphic organizer; it may be the choice of transition words, or it may be their opening paragraph. Only point out examples that reflect one of these learned skills.

Structured Practice: Ask students what they expressed as being their ideal job. Comment on their choices. List students' choice of jobs. Next, ask why students picked these occupations as their ideal jobs. This will be the basis of their three reasons why they picked this particular job. Again, circulate the classroom and ask students for just one reason why they picked this particular job as an ideal one. Again, list each of their first reasons for picking this job.

Guided Practice: Show your sample of your ideal job. As indicated on your G.O., give your first reason why you picked this as an ideal job. Explain to students that first you will tell your reason, next explain your reason and then back it up with supporting details and a personal experience or a story. Leave your sample on the board. Tell students that they will now write their second paragraph or first reason why they would consider this to be their ideal job. Circulate the classroom and allow students time to first check their graphic organizers why they picked this as an ideal job. Next, have students follow their graphic organizer for reason one (like yourself) and write five to six sentences to support their first reason. Circulate the classroom and offer help if necessary.

This is your time to encourage, praise and give support!

My ideal job would be a teacher

One reason

Mrs. Smith

A teacher in Virginia

Dreams

Put my mind to it

Other teachers helped me

One reason *I have chosen to become a teacher is because I am a product of someone whom I consider to be the best teacher in the world. As a child from Virginia, I was inspired by a wonderful coach and teacher named Mrs. Smith. Mrs. Smith taught me that any dream was possible. If I put my mind to accomplishing any goal I could make it happen. Mrs. Smith inspired me to be the best I could be at anything I wanted to be. Through my childhood and into my adult life I have had other important teachers who encouraged me to carry out my dreams. These wonderful exciting people in my life have helped me in my decision to become a teacher.*

DAY 23

Standard: The student will write a draft appropriate to the topic, audience and purpose.

Objective: The student will learn how to write the third paragraph in an expository essay.

Night Writes: Ask 3 students to share their Night Writes™ journal entry with the class. Post Night Writes™ topic for homework.

Word of the Day: Have students find the "Word of the Day" in the dictionary, copy the definition, and write a complete sentence using the word. Ask several students to read their sentences.

Review: The introduction and second paragraph have been completed. Pick three or four students to share their ideal job and their first reason why they considered this career as their ideal job.

Skill Introduction: Paragraph 3 will discuss or explain the second reason why you considered a certain career as your ideal job.

Modeling: Think out loud. Orally read your second paragraph to the class again. Explain that this is your first main idea (reason) why you picked a teacher as an ideal job. Explain to students that you will now move to paragraph 3 or your second reason why you picked this as your ideal job. Point out to students that the process is quite methodical. You will check off each step as you complete it on your G.O. Read your second reason why you picked being a teacher as your ideal job.

Structured Practice: Again, ask different students what they expressed as being their ideal job on their Graphic Organizer (G.O.) Comment on their choices. Ask selected students to read their first reason for picking this particular job. Comment accordingly. Allow other students to comment on the other students' reasons as well. Again, circulate the classroom and list second reasons for picking this job.

Guided Practice: Show your sample of your ideal job. As indicated on your graphic organizer, give your second reason why you picked this as an ideal job. Explain to students that again you will tell your reason, next explain your reason and then back it up with supporting details and a personal experience or a story. Leave your sample on the board. Tell students that they will now write their third paragraph or second reason why they would consider this to be their ideal job. Circulate the classroom and allow students time to first, check their graphic organizers why they considered this career as an ideal job. Next, have students follow their G.O. for reason two (like yourself) and write five to six sentences to support their second reason. Circulate the classroom and offer help if necessary.

This is your time to encourage, praise and give support! Orally comment on students who are exhibiting excellent writing and reasoning.

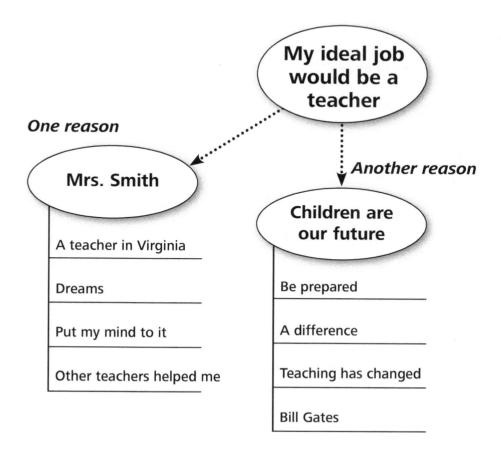

One reason

My ideal job would be a teacher

Mrs. Smith

A teacher in Virginia

Dreams

Put my mind to it

Other teachers helped me

Another reason

Children are our future

Be prepared

A difference

Teaching has changed

Bill Gates

Another reason why teaching would be an ideal job is because our children are our future. Teaching makes a difference in them because it gives them tools to help them be successful in the future. As the century has changed so has the method of communication. As Bill Gates says, "I'm very optimistic about what we will see not just in the next ten years but over the next year." I want to be a part of this process and what better way than that of a teacher.

DAY 24

Standard: The student will write a draft appropriate to the topic, audience and purpose.

Objective: The student will learn how to write the fourth paragraph in an expository essay.

Night Writes: Ask three students to share their Night Writes™ journal entry with the class. Post Night Writes™ topic for homework.

Word of the Day: Have students find the "Word of the Day" in the dictionary, copy the definition, and write a complete sentence using the word. Ask several students to read their sentences.

Review: The introduction (first paragraph), second and third paragraph have been completed. Pick three or four students to share their ideal job and their second reason why they considered this career as their ideal job.

Skill Introduction: Paragraph 4 will discuss or explain the third reason why you picked a certain career as your ideal job.

Modeling: *Think out loud.* Orally read your third paragraph to the class again. Explain that this is your second reason why you picked a teacher as an ideal job. Explain to students that you will now move to paragraph 4 or your third reason why you picked this as your ideal job. Point out to students that the process is quite methodical. You will check off each step as you complete it on your Graphic Organizer G.O. Read your third reason why you picked being a teacher as your ideal job.

Structured Practice: Again, ask different students what they expressed as being their ideal job on their G.O. Comment on their choices. Ask selected students what their second reason was for picking this particular job. Have them read their paragraphs and comment accordingly. Allow other students to comment on their reasons as well.

Guided Practice: Show your sample of your ideal job. As indicated on your graphic organizer, give your third reason why you picked this as an ideal job. Explain to students that again you will tell your reason, explain your reason and then back it up with supporting details and a personal experience or a story. Leave your sample on the board. Tell students that they will now write their fourth paragraph or third reason why they would consider this to be their ideal job. Circulate the classroom and allow students time to first, check their G.O.'s why they considered this career as an ideal job. Next, have students follow their G.O. for reason three (like yourself) and write five to six sentences that support their third reason. Circulate the classroom and offer help if necessary.

> *This is your time to encourage, praise and give support! Orally comment on students who are exhibiting excellent writing and reasoning.*

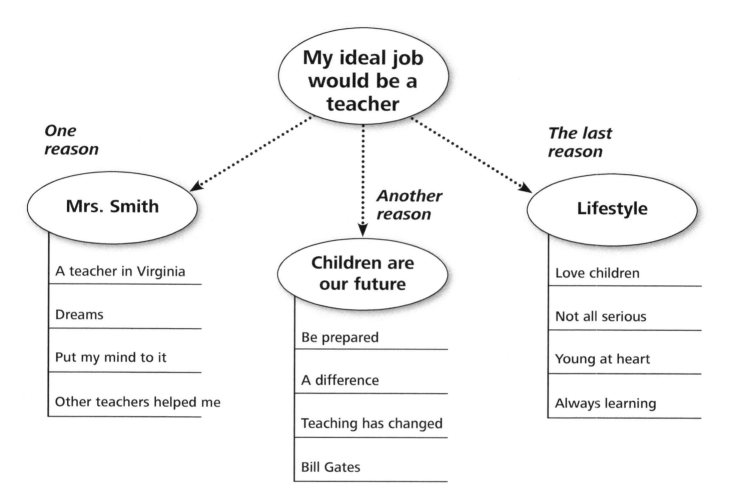

One reason

My ideal job would be a teacher

Mrs. Smith

A teacher in Virginia

Dreams

Put my mind to it

Other teachers helped me

Another reason

Children are our future

Be prepared

A difference

Teaching has changed

Bill Gates

The last reason

Lifestyle

Love children

Not all serious

Young at heart

Always learning

The last reason why a teacher would be an ideal job for me is that I like the lifestyle that a teacher lives. I could not imagine myself behind a desk all day. I love to be around children and to be a part of their growing up. Children are so uncanny and naïve that it helps me to remember that life does not have to be completely serious. I cannot imagine another job that would keep me young at heart. Not only do I like the fact that children keep you young, but a career in teaching does not end your education. The methods in which you perform your job are always changing. Teachers are never done learning, always adapting a point of view, and using their imagination constantly.

DAY 25

Standard: The student will write a draft appropriate to the topic, audience and purpose.

Objective: The student will learn how to write the fifth or closing paragraph in an expository essay.

Night Writes: Ask three students to share their Night Writes™ journal entry with the class. Post Night Writes™ topic for homework.

Word of the Day: Have students find the "Word of the Day" in the dictionary, copy the definition, and write a complete sentence using the word. Ask several students to read their sentences.

Review: The introduction (first paragraph), second, third and fourth paragraph have been completed. Pick three or four students to share their ideal job and their third reason why they considered this career as their ideal job.

Skill Introduction: Paragraph 5 will be the conclusion for the expository essay. It should be a summary of the reasons why the student picked a certain career as their ideal job.

Modeling: *Think out loud.* Orally read your fourth paragraph to the class again. Explain that this is your third reason why you picked a teacher as an ideal job. Explain to students that you will now move to paragraph 5 or your conclusion. Explain that the conclusion is the final part that summarizes your main points. It should restate the main points but not in the same words. Point out to students that the process is quite methodical. You will check off each step as you complete it on your G.O. Read your conclusion.

Structured Practice: Again, ask different students what they expressed as being their ideal job on their G.O. Comment on their choices. Ask selected students what their third reason was for picking this particular job. Have them read their paragraphs and comment accordingly. Allow other students to comment on their reasons as well.

Guided Practice: Show your sample of your ideal job. As indicated on your graphic organizer, give your example of the conclusion. See suggested words that students can use as ways to begin their conclusion. Leave your sample on the board. Tell students that they will now write their conclusion by using one of the words listed to begin their final paragraph. Circulate the classroom and allow students time to first, check their G.O.'s for the reasons why they considered this career as an ideal job. Next, have students follow their G.O. for the conclusion and write at least two convincing sentences that summarizes why this is an ideal job for them. The conclusion should restate the three reasons why the student picked this occupation as their ideal job.

This is your time to encourage, praise and give support! Orally comment on students who are exhibiting excellent writing and reasoning.

after all	all in all	all things considered
in conclusion	on the whole	in short
in summary	to summarize	in the final analysis
in the long run	on balance	to sum up
to summarize	finally	in fact
surely	obviously	definitely
in effect	as a result of	altogether
indeed	overall	for these reasons
certainly	consequently	in other words

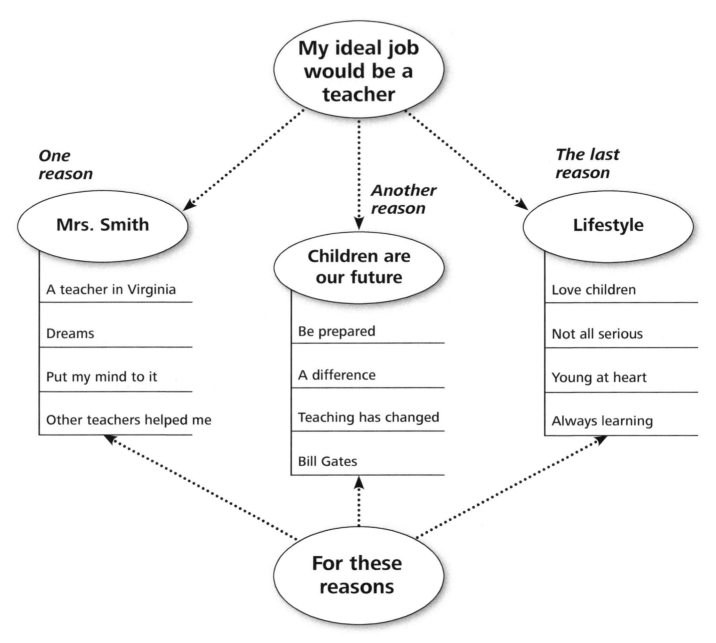

My ideal job would be a teacher

One reason

Mrs. Smith

A teacher in Virginia

Dreams

Put my mind to it

Other teachers helped me

Another reason

Children are our future

Be prepared

A difference

Teaching has changed

Bill Gates

The last reason

Lifestyle

Love children

Not all serious

Young at heart

Always learning

For these reasons

For these reasons, choosing a career in teaching is the most important job that I could hold. Influential people like Mrs. Smith have led me to believe that teachers can make a difference in a child's life. Teachers are the people who produce future doctors, lawyers, politicians, and other various important people that make our society as powerful as it is today. And, finally, as I am one who loves a challenge and change, it is a lifestyle that would be ideal for me.

How do people decide what an ideal job would be? I have always known I wanted to be a teacher. I have many people who have influenced my life choices and many fond memories to validate I am making the right choices. To me, being a teacher is not only my ideal job, but it is a quality that is imprinted in my heart.

One reason I have chosen to become a teacher is because I am a product of someone whom I consider to be the best teacher in the world. As a child in Virginia, I was inspired by a wonderful coach and teacher named Mrs. Smith. Mrs. Smith taught me that any dream was possible. If I put my mind to accomplishing any goal I could make it happen. Mrs. Smith inspired me to be the best I could be at anything I wanted to be. Through my childhood and into my adult life I have had other important teachers who encouraged me to carry out my dreams. These wonderful exciting people in my life have helped me in my decision to become a teacher.

Another reason why teaching would be an ideal job is because our children are our future. Teaching makes a difference in them because it gives them tools to help them be successful in the future. As the century has changed so has the method of communication. As Bill Gates says, "I'm very optimistic about what we will see not just in the next ten years but over the next year." I want to be a part of this process and what better way than that of a teacher.

The last reason why a teacher would be an ideal job for me is that I like the lifestyle that a teacher lives. I could not imagine myself behind a desk all day. I love to be around children and to be a part of their growing up. Children are so uncanny and naïve that it helps me to remember that life does not have to be completely serious. I cannot imagine another job that would keep me young at heart. Not only do I like the fact that children keep you young, but a career in teaching does not end your education. The methods in which you perform your job are always changing. Teachers are never done learning, always adapting a point of view, and using their imagination constantly.

For these reasons, choosing a career in teaching is the most important job that I could hold. Influential people like Mrs. Smith have led me to believe that teachers can make a difference in a child's life. Teachers are the people who produce future doctors, lawyers, politicians, and other various important people that make our society as powerful as it is today. And, finally, as I am one who loves a challenge and change, it is a lifestyle that would be ideal for me.

DAY 26

Standard: The student will write a draft appropriate to the topic, audience and purpose.

Objective: The student will learn how to write their first expository essay independently.

Night Writes: Ask 3 students to share their Night Writes™ journal entry with the class. Post "Night Writes™" topic for homework.

Word of the Day: Have students find the "Word of the Day" in the dictionary, copy the definition, and write a complete sentence using the word. Ask several students to read their sentences.

Review: The G.O. and its three components: circle the topic, draw a rectangle around the clue word(s), and underline what the student is to write about. Use examples for review. Review the five parts of the expository essay. Review samples of introductions (first paragraph), three main ideas (reasons) with details (second, third and fourth paragraphs) and the closing (fifth paragraph). At this point, you may wish to have 3 or 4 students share their ideal job and give an example of a concluding paragraph.

Independent Practice: Assure students that this is a practice. Students will be given 45 minutes to plan a G.O. (graphic organizer) and write a 5 paragraph essay on the topic below. Explain that students may use all reference materials (either their notes or the four displayed posters which include an outline of a five paragraph essay, the nine types of great grabbers, transition words, and cool conclusions.

Sometimes keeping a good friend can be harder than making a new friend.

Before you begin writing, think about how to keep a good friend.

Now explain to the reader how to keep a good friend.

Standard: The student will develop and use a classroom rubric for written work and use for peer review and editing.

Objective: The student will learn how to understand the writing rubric and how an essay is scored.

Night Writes: Ask 3 students to share their Night Writes™ journal entry with the class. Post "Night Writes™" topic for homework.

Word of the Day: Have students find the "Word of the Day" in the dictionary, copy the definition, and write a complete sentence using the word. Ask several students to read their sentences.

Review: The purpose of the expository essay is to explain, define, inform, instruct, or clarify. These are the CodeBreakers™. Ensure that students understand what these words mean. See attached sample. Have students write the CodeBreakers™ in their Writer's Notebook under "Notes". Next have students write a sentence using these five CodeBreakers™.

Skill Introduction: Students will learn about the scoring guide (or rubric) for writing.

Modeling: Explain to students that a rubric is a scoring guide. It tells the teacher and the student what parts of their essay will be evaluated. To determine a grade, essays are judged on the following four writing elements: focus, organization, support and conventions. Place the attached sample on the overhead. Reinforce the thought that good expository is full of information, descriptions, reasons, and supporting details.

Structured Practice: C stands for concentrate (focus), **A** stands for arrange (organize), **S** stands for supporting details, and **L** stands for language. Now ask individual students to repeat what each of the letters stand for. Go over what each of these four elements of writing means. Ask individual students to repeat the description of these four elements. To further reinforce the four elements, call out one of the four letters and have a student stand up and tell you the word and what it means. Repeat this exercise several times. Briefly discuss the scale of scoring – high, medium, and low. A more comprehensive discussion will follow (See attached sample).

Guided Practice: Have students turn to the section titled, "Scoring" in the Writer's Notebook. Have students write out the definitions of the four elements. Circulate about the classroom and praise students who are following directions. Help those students who are having difficulty completing this assignment. Upon completion of this portion of the assignment, place examples of several essays (see samples) on the overhead. Have students read aloud and, as a class, score them as low (0-2), medium (3-4), or high (5-6). At this point, the class is judging if they have the four elements of an expository essay.

Independent Practice: Have students complete their own G.O.'s on the following subject. Explain that if practiced on a continuing basis, students can increase their speed which will allow more time for them to write their essay. Have students circle, underline and draw a rectangle as instructed in previous lessons. The objective is to complete a G.O. in less than ten minutes. The writing prompt is as follows:

Everyone would like to receive straight A's in school.

Before you begin writing, think about why it is important to get good grades.

Now explain why making good grades is important.

Upon completion, collect G.O.'s from the students to review and return on the following day.

CodeBreakers™

Explain — to tell how to do something

Define — to make clear the meaning of an idea

Inform — to give facts about an idea

Instruct — to teach something

Clarify — to explain clearly

C A S L

C oncentrate – focus on the main idea

A rrange – a plan with a beginning, middle and end

S upporting Details – examples and reasons; vivid verbs, juicy words, and words of the day

L anguage – capitalization, spelling, punctuation, and sentence structure

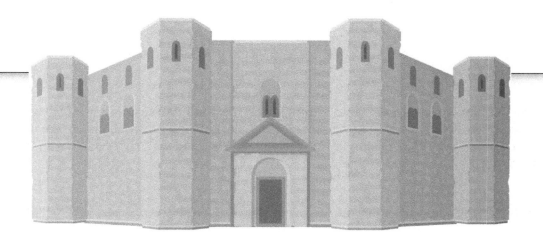

Writing Topic:

Everyone has a favorite person.

Think about reasons why this individual is your favorite person.

Explain why he or she is your favorite person.

Essay 1:

Everyone has someone to like right? I like someone her name is Carrie. I like her because she is fun, is a good friend, and she is not bossy.

First, I like her because she is fun. She always play with me. Sometimes she lets me chose what to do. Carrie does not play rough with me.

Second, she is a good friend. She is very nice. Carrie is not mean to me and I get along good.

Next, she is never bossy to me. She does not tell my what to do. She never yells at me or also not get in hand fight or word fights.

Last, Carries fun, she is a good friend and she is not bossy that is why I like her.

Scoring:

Concentrate _____ Arrange _____ Supporting Details _____ Language _____

Essay 2:

Everyone has you person to vote. Tell you a person that I like.

The person that I like is my mom because she takes me on ride to Disnay land the paaaark and somewere to eat like Gran buffay and we eat pizza, and ice crem and wee Movie's of the movie's like spierman, and Man in Black II and we run buy me YU-Gi-of cards, buy toy's for my little brothr, and, buy movie's

And that why I like my mom because she is the baest's mom in the wrod.

Scoring:

Concentrate _____ Arrange _____ Supporting Details _____ Language _____

Essay 3:

Everyone likes someone even me I like Sammi in real life. But I don't know how to tell her she probly Don't like me, but I don't care. I like her because she charmin and pretty all at one. I'm not ling about it I like her if you don't so what. As long as you don't tell no one, and I like Mary the same way, but I still want to go out with Sammi.

Scoring:

Concentrate _____ Arrange _____ Supporting Details _____ Language _____

Essay 4:

I like this person becues she is pruety. This person like me and I like her. This person like me for a freind. This person name is Sue. I like her becues she is pruety and she is cout. She is freindley and she is niest to peoples.

Scoring:

Concentrate _____ Arrange _____ Supporting Details _____ Language _____

Essay 5:

I have many friends. Out of all of the special persons the one I want to write about is Miss Jones. She is my fourth grade teacher. Miss Jones is a kind teacher. She works very hard. I like her. I wish she could be my teacher forever.

Miss jones is always there when I need her I can always count on her. She is someone I can trust.

Last, she is my wonderful 4th grade teacher. She works so hard. She is just so wonderful.

She is just the greatist. I love having her for ma teacher. She deserves all the thanks she can get.

Scoring:

Concentrate _____ Arrange _____ Supporting Details _____ Language _____

Essay 6:

Hey! do you have a special person that you like? Well, I do and his name is Ken and he is my brother. I like my brother because he is nice, playful and helps me out with things. I will tell you why I like him the most.

I like my brother the most because he is very nice. He never hits me. Chase me with or knife or trips me and starts to laughs. He never does any of those things because he is a nice brother.

The second reason why I like him is that he is playful. He always plays with me after my homwork. We play games like football, baseball, basketball and catch we play more games but those are just some of them.

The third thing is he helps me out with things. Things like making things, drawings and stuff and when I am sick he get me ice creeem. There are some other things but those are just some things he does.

So those were all the things that I like my brother for. And they were he is very nice, he plays with me very day and he helps me out. So those were all the reasons I like my brother.

Scoring:

Concentrate _____ Arrange _____ Supporting Details _____ Language _____

Essay 7:

My brother is my bast brother, but he play with me. He like to play ball. I like my brther.

Scoring:

Concentrate _____ Arrange _____ Supporting Details _____ Language _____

Essay 8:

"Who is your favorite person?" Jamping Jaguars you don't know? Well grab a blanket and some hot chocolate and I will tell you what my favorite person is. My favorite person is my mom.

One reason why my mom is my favorite person is because my mom is nice. She will take me shopping if I am good and behave.

The next reason why I like my mom is because she's thankful and considerant. Then she will let my friends stay over if I had very good grades like A's. B's, and C's. I like my mom because she will take me to a store like Walmart or Kmart. Also I went to TGI Fridays every Friday.

The third reason is that she will take me to a good restraurnt or a good fast food place to eat at. My favirate restraint is TGI Fridays. I like cold ice teas that are in a glass cup. Then I like there hamburgers, and there chicken nuggets and there french fries.

Finally, the last reason is that I like my mom because she is nice, and she will take me shopping if I am good and behaved. And she take me out to eat at my favorite reastraunt. Then she is very concederent to people. But most of all I lover her because she is my favorite person and she loves me and I lover her.

But I hoped you enjoyed my story and know I told you who is my favirate person and I gave you all my reasons.

Scoring:

Concentrate _____ Arrange _____ Supporting Details _____ Language _____

Essay 9:

Have you ever thought about a person you really like? Well, I'd like t tell you about mine, but first let me tell you who he is. My favorite person is my dad. I want to tell you three things about him. He is kind, he is funny, and he's a family guy. Now let me start my story.

First, he is very, very kind to my sisters, my friends, and mostly everyone else he meets. Then most people see him for the first time, this happens to most of my friends, they think he is going to be really mean. Like if he was going to boss people or have a really bad temper or something like that. But once they got to know him they said he was really nice. It's nice to have a dad like that.

Second, my dad can be very funny. He loves to tell jokes to everyone. For example, once while my dad was having lunch, with my friend Brittany, at school, he told us some jokes, like what do you call cheese that's not yours? Nacho cheese. Get it.

Third, my dad is a family guy for lots of reasons. For one he's kind and funny in many ways. And he's also making us feel proud of ourselves. He's always bragging about my sisters and I like when he says "My daughters are going to become a lawyer or doctor and have a great life."

So, do you understand why I like my dad so much? I feel so lucky to have my dad. If you don't have a dad you're missing out on all the fun. And trust me, it's not bad being without a dad. I mean, it's not like you don't have anyone to turn to.

Scoring:

Concentrate _____ Arrange _____ Supporting Details _____ Language _____

Standard: The student will develop and use a classroom rubric for written work and use for peer review and editing.

Objective: The student will learn how to understand the writing rubric and how an essay is scored.

Night Writes: Ask 3 students to share their Night Writes™ journal entry with the class. Post "Night Writes™" topic for homework.

Word of the Day: Have students find the "Word of the Day" in the dictionary, copy the definition, and write a complete sentence using the word. Ask several students to read their sentences.

Review: CASL stands for Concentrate, Arrange, Supporting Details and Language. Concentrate is to focus on the topic; Arrange is to have a plan; Support is the use of details to explain, clarify or define. Language uses correct punctuation, capitalization, spelling and sentence structure. Have students orally reiterate the four elements of good writing.

Skill Introduction: Students will continue to learn about the scoring guide (or rubric) for writing.

Modeling: Give details what constitutes a good piece of expository writing. Discuss that good expository writing must be full of information, description, reasons, and supporting detail. Explain that a rubric is a scoring guide. Place the rubric on the overhead and examine each of the various levels pointing out that the higher the score, the better the essay. Explain to students that you will not accept anything less than a 4 on future essays. "Four is more!"

Structured Practice: Point to the rubric and have various students read the scoring guide. Ask students if it is better to receive a high number or a low number on a test. Have them explain their reasons. At this stage, it is important for students to fully understand what represents an acceptable essay.

Guided Practice: Distribute the numbers 0, 1, and 2 cut out of black construction paper. Explain that black numbers denote bad scores. Have students glue each of these numbers on a separate sheet of paper in their "Writer's Notebook". Have students follow your sample and write down exactly what each of these 3 black numbers mean. Next distribute the numbers 3, 4, 5 and 6 cut out of white construction paper. Explain that students will have the opportunity to color these numbers after each number is glued on a separate piece of paper and discussed in detail. Explain that the higher the number, the more colorful the number.

Independent Practice: Distribute students' graphic organizers that were completed on the following topic yesterday.

Everyone would like to receive straight A's in school.

Before you begin writing, think about why it is important to get good grades.

Now explain why making good grades is important.

Tell students that they will now write their opening paragraph which must use one of the nine great grabbers to capture the reader's attention. Remind students that they are free to use their "Writer's Notebook" as a reference.

Allow students ten minutes to complete this opening paragraph. Explain to students that soon they will be able to complete the opening paragraph in less than five minutes. Upon completion, collect papers and review for your own edification.

0 Unscorable

Can't read

Way off topic

No words

1 Poor

No focus –way off topic

No organization

No transition words

Lots of grammar mistakes

Hard to read

Incomplete sentences

No supporting ideas or details

Listing with no explanation

No juicy words

2 Low

Slightly relevant

Little information on the topic

Poorly organized

Few transition words

Simple sentence structure

Few supporting ideas – only 1 or 2 details in most paragraphs

Limited word choice

Few juicy words

3 Average

Information is on topic

Has an attempted organizational pattern

Missing some transition words

Mostly complete sentences with a simple sentence structure

Some capitalization, punctuation, grammar and spelling errors

Some supporting ideas and details – 3 in most paragraphs

Word choice is predictable but uses some juicy words

4 Getting There

More information on the topic

Pattern is established

Shows more arrangement

Transitions are used

Uses complete sentences and varied sentence structure

Few capitalization, punctuation, grammar and spelling errors

Supporting ideas developed with more details

Adequate word choice

Good use of juicy words

5 More Interesting

Focused – almost there!

Lots more information on the topic

Pattern is established with few lapses

Shows lots more arrangement

Transitions are used

Sentences are complete and sentence structure is varied

Very few capitalization, punctuation, grammar and spelling errors

Good supporting details

Adequate word choice

Interesting use of juicy words

6 Outstanding

All sentences on topic

Logically arranged in order

Sense of completeness of the entire essay

Transitions are used

Sentences are complete and structure is varied

No capitalization, punctuation, grammar and spelling errors

Excellent development of supporting ideas

Precise word choice

Precise choice of juicy words

Standard: The student will use prewriting strategies to generate ideas and formulate a plan.

Objective: The student will be able to identify the structural elements of each paragraph using the graphic organizer as a guide.

Night Writes: Ask 3 students to share their Night Writes™ journal entry with the class. Post "Night Writes™" topic for homework.

Word of the Day: Have students find the "Word of the Day" in the dictionary, copy the definition, and write a complete sentence using the word. Ask several students to read their sentences.

Review: Have students turn to the "Scoring" section of their Writer's Notebook. Review the scoring in detail to ensure that all students understand how their papers will be graded.

Skill Introduction: Students will be able to identify the structural elements of each paragraph using the graphic organizer as a guide.

Modeling: Walk students through the G.O. as a structural guide to writing for expository writing. Discuss each of the five paragraphs.

>   **Introduction:** Two parts – an interesting grabber to catch the reader's attention (the hook!) and a topic sentence that briefly and clearly states what this piece of writing is going to be about. It also states the three main ideas of the essay.

>   **Body:** The body is made up of three paragraphs. Each paragraph contains a main idea that explains what the paragraph is about and includes at least 3 to 4 supporting details per paragraph.

>   **Conclusion:** The final paragraph begins with a cool conclusion word and then summarizes the three reasons and restates the topic.

Structured Practice: Display the attached essay sample, "The Discovery of Foods." Read it aloud and have students identify the structural elements of each paragraph, using the graphic organizer as a guide. Work together to complete an analysis of "The Discovery of Foods" by responding to the questions. This activity demonstrates the process of paragraph analysis to the class. Tasks include:

- *Numbering the paragraphs*
- *Labeling the introduction and conclusion*
- *Underlining the main ideas in paragraphs 2, 3, and 4*
- *Summarizing the information in these paragraphs*
- *Listing supporting details*
- *Locating specific information within the paragraphs*
- *Summarizing the topic*

Independent Practice: Distribute students' graphic organizers along with their opening paragraphs that were completed on the following topic yesterday.

- *Everyone would like to receive straight A's in school.*
- *Before you begin writing, think about why it is important to get good grades.*
- *Now explain why making good grades is important.*

Tell students that they will now write their second and third paragraph which must include at least three supporting details for each of the two main ideas. Remind students that they are free to use their "Writer's Notebook" as a reference.

Allow students twenty minutes to complete these next two paragraphs. Explain to students that soon they will be able to complete these two paragraphs in less than fifteen minutes. Upon completion, collect papers and review for your own edification.

Have you ever wondered where all those new foods on the supermarket shelf come from? Hundreds of new foods are created every year, and each one is the result of an inventor at work. Potato chips, chewing gum, and peanut butter are three popular foods that were invented here in North America.

Today, potato chips are the biggest selling snack food in the United States. The average American eats about 4 pounds of potato chips every year. Sometime inventions happen by accident. This is how the potato chip was invented about 150 years ago by a chef named George Crumb. One night a customer at the restaurant asked George to make the potatoes thinner and George cut them as thin as paper and fried them in oil. The customer loved them and the idea soon caught on. It wasn't until a potato peeling machine was invented that potato chips could be made in factories and sold all over North America.

Imagine a chewing gum made from tree sap. The earliest chewing gum was invented by the African people, who used the resin from the black spruce tree for a kind of chewy snack. The African people shared this idea with the pioneers who settled in North America. In 1850, John Curtis decided to turn this idea into a chewing gum business. He cooked the gum until it was thick, rolled it out, and cut it into small pieces. They called it "pure spruce gum".

It's hard to believe that four out of every five homes in the United States has peanut butter in their cupboards. Peanut butter was invented by a doctor from St. Louis, Missouri. He wanted to give his patients a high protein food that was easy to digest. It contains lots of protein, vitamins and minerals. Now there are lots of factories that make peanut butter and this food is the most common sandwich filling in children's lunches.

Food is always changing thanks to inventors who continue to think up new foods. So go ahead, crunch that potato chip, chew that gum and spread the peanut butter. Perhaps someday you will create a food of your own.

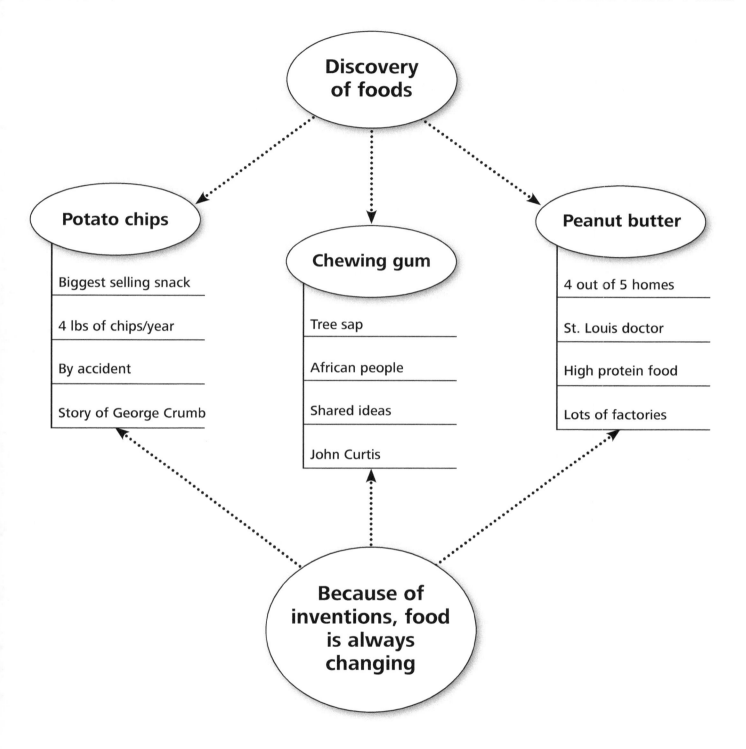

Discovery of foods

Potato chips

Biggest selling snack

4 lbs of chips/year

By accident

Story of George Crumb

Chewing gum

Tree sap

African people

Shared ideas

John Curtis

Peanut butter

4 out of 5 homes

St. Louis doctor

High protein food

Lots of factories

Because of inventions, food is always changing

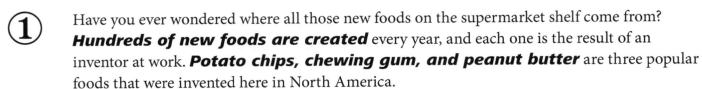

Introduction

① Have you ever wondered where all those new foods on the supermarket shelf come from? ***Hundreds of new foods are created*** every year, and each one is the result of an inventor at work. ***Potato chips, chewing gum, and peanut butter*** are three popular foods that were invented here in North America.

② Today, ***potato chips*** are the biggest selling snack food in the United States. The average American eats about 4 pounds of potato chips every year. Sometime inventions happen by accident. This is how the potato chip was invented about 150 years ago by a chef named George Crumb. One night a customer at the restaurant asked George to make the potatoes thinner and George cut them as thin as paper and fried them in oil. The customer loved them and the idea soon caught on. It wasn't until a potato peeling machine was invented that potato chips could be made in factories and sold all over North America.

③ Imagine a ***chewing gum*** made from tree sap. The earliest chewing gum was invented by the African people, who used the resin from the black spruce tree for a kind of chewy snack. The African people shared this idea with the pioneers who settled in North America. In 1850, John Curtis decided to turn this idea into a chewing gum business. He cooked the gum until it was thick, rolled it out, and cut it into small pieces. They called it "pure spruce gum".

④ It's hard to believe that four out of every five homes in the United States has peanut butter in their cupboards. ***Peanut butter*** was invented by a doctor from St. Louis, Missouri. He wanted to give his patients a high protein food that was easy to digest. It contains lots of protein, vitamins and minerals. Now there are lots of factories that make peanut butter and this food is the most common sandwich filling in children's lunches.

Conclusion

⑤ Food is always changing thanks to inventors who continue to think up new foods. So go ahead, crunch that potato chip, chew that gum and spread the peanut butter. Perhaps someday you will create a food of your own.

Standard: The student will use prewriting strategies to generate ideas and formulate a plan.

Objective: The student will be able to identify the structural elements of each paragraph using the graphic organizer as a guide.

Night Writes: Ask 3 students to share their Night Writes™ journal entry with the class. Post "Night Writes™" topic for homework.

Word of the Day: Have students find the "Word of the Day" in the dictionary, copy the definition, and write a complete sentence using the word. Ask several students to read their sentences.

Review: Again, review the four writing elements and CodeBreakers™. Call on four individual students to describe the writing elements. Have them stand and explain as you call out the various letters. **C** = Concentrate (clear main idea); **A** = Arrange (a plan, logical ideas, paragraphs and transitions); **S**= Support (quality of details); **L** = Language (Punctuation, Capitalization, Spelling, and Sentence Structure). Repeat this exercise with four other students. Continue the repetition until all students have had an opportunity to respond. Have students open their writing notebooks to the section titled "Scoring". Ask what number represents an acceptable paper. Reiterate that "4 is More" and soon all students will be at this level.

Skill Introduction: Students will be able to set goals and monitor the progress of their expository writing essays.

Modeling: Place the progress chart on the overhead. Explain that the first writing test will be given tomorrow. Based on the Writing Rubric that students copied on Day 28, they will predict a realistic goal for their first official graded test. Make sure that the rubric is posted in the room as well. In that manner, students can understand how they can predict their score. As a teacher, you may say that after 5 weeks of instruction, you can make a 4 because . . . and list what comprises a 4. Then have students color the first bar in up to the number 4 on the chart (See attached sample).

Structured Practice. Hand out a chart to all students. Have them review their writing rubric in their notebook. Also have students look at your posted rubric (which should match their writing rubric in their Writer's Notebook). After orally reviewing the rubric with students, call on various students to announce their predictions and their reasoning for selecting this number. Following a question and answer session, have students draw a horizontal line and color in their goal for the first official test. Circulate the room to ensure students are graphing it correctly.

TEST TOMORROW!

Independent Practice: Distribute students' graphic organizers along with their first, second and third paragraphs that were completed on the following topic for the past two sessions.

Everyone would like to receive straight A's in school.

Before you begin writing, think about why it is important to get good grades.

Now explain why making good grades is important.

Tell students that they will now write their fourth paragraph which must include at least three supporting details for the main idea of paragraph four. The last paragraph (paragraph 5) must summarize the topic and the three main ideas presented in paragraphs 2, 3 and 4. Remind students that they are free to use their "Writer's Notebook" as a reference.

Allow students twenty minutes to complete the two remaining paragraphs. Explain to students that soon they will be able to complete these last two paragraphs in less than fifteen minutes. Upon completion, collect papers and review for your own edification.

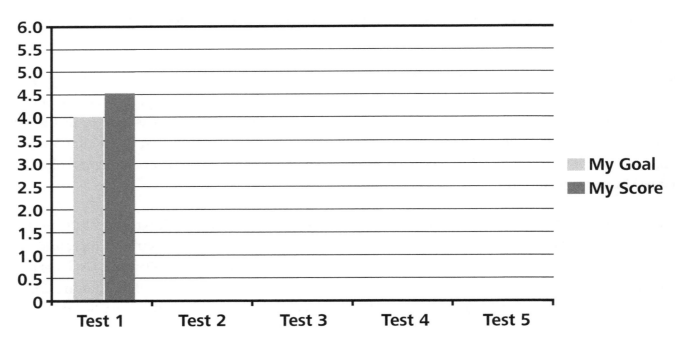

My Progress on Expository Writing Tests

Standard: The student will write a draft appropriate to the topic, audience and purpose.

Objective: The student will learn how to write their second expository essay independently.

Night Writes: Ask 3 students to share their Night Writes™ journal entry with the class. Post "Night Writes™" topic for homework.

Word of the Day: Have students find the "Word of the Day" in the dictionary, copy the definition, and write a complete sentence using the word. Ask several students to read their sentences.

Review: Review the graphic organizer and its three components: circle the topic, draw a rectangle around the clue word(s), and underline what the student is to write about. Use examples for review. Review the five parts of the expository essay. Review the introduction (first paragraph), three main ideas (reasons) with details (second, third and fourth paragraphs) and the closing (fifth paragraph). At this point, share selected pieces of student writing that demonstrates excellence from the completion of past topic. Students love to receive praise!

Independent Practice: Explain to students that this is their first official test. Students will be given 45 minutes to plan a graphic organizer (G.O.) and write a 5 paragraph essay on the topic below. Remind students of the goals they set yesterday. Review the scoring and ensure that the writing rubric is posted in the room.

> *Most of us have someone that we deeply admire. Sometimes we wonder what it would be like to be that person.*
>
> *Before you begin writing, think about a person you admire.*
>
> *Now write to explain why you would like to be that person for a day.*

Teacher Notes: Yes! You are now going to have to grade your students' essays! The first graded essay may take you a bit more time until you get use to the process. Grade the students' essays by breaking it down in the four elements : **Concentrate, Arrange, Supporting Details and Language.**

Based on the rubric, give them a score between 0 and 6 for each element. Next average the four scores and give one grade. Write a positive comment regarding this first independent attempt. For this first graded essay, **do not criticize too deeply.** I have found that students gain confidence if you point out their strengths.

Now here is the key to have your students performing beyond their expectations. Go through the essays and pick out papers that have a great graphic organizer (G.O.), great grabber, great use of vocabulary, great title, great use of personal experiences, great use of action verbs, great use of transition words, great use of detail, great simile, great color word, great alliteration, great ending. . . anything that will encourage them to write even better. Encourage these writing techniques. Trust me. The time you spend on taking this additional initiative will pay you back tenfold! Take those examples and write them on a separate sheet of paper. You will use these examples in tomorrow's lesson.

DAY 32

Standard: The student will use supporting ideas, details, and facts from a variety of sources to develop and elaborate the topic.

Objective: The student will be able to identify the structural elements of each paragraph using the graphic organizer as a guide.

Night Writes: Ask 3 students to share their Night Writes™ journal entry with the class. Post "Night Writes™" topic for homework.

Word of the Day: Have students find the "Word of the Day" in the dictionary, copy the definition, and write a complete sentence using the word. Ask several students to read their sentences.

Review: Review the four writing elements: Concentrate, Arrange, Supporting Details and Language. Explain that for a paper to score at least a 3 or 4 they must have all of these elements in their writing essay. Review the writing rubric. Have students pull out their progress chart that charted their goal for yesterday's writing test. Distribute students' graded essays. Next, have students chart their exact score next to their goal in another color. Ask students how close they came with their goals. How many were right on target? How many were below? How many were above? Have students place their first official graded paper under "Tests" in their Writer's Notebook.

Skill Introduction: Students will be able to understand what elements make up an excellent expository essay. Students will also learn how details play a key element in the writing process.

Modeling: From yesterday's graded essays, read the selections that demonstrate great writing. Cite the students' names and praise them for their excellent writing skills. If there is a student who used a simile in the writing test, make sure that you show this example. Following the examples, introduce the word simile. Explain to students that this is just one writing skill that helps enhance details. Write the definition of simile on the overhead. Have students copy the definition and place in their Writer's Notebook under the heading, "Notes". The definition of a simile is a comparison between two things using like and as. Give the following examples of similes:

- *He ran as fast as a cheetah.*

- *My hair looks like flowing ocean waves after midnight.*

- *My hands are as rough as skin of a crocodile.*

Pick random things in the class and model to students how to create a simile with a specific object. For example,

- *The chair is as strong as Superman.*

- *Her lips are as red as cherries.*

Structured Practice: Have students copy down the above examples in their Writer's Notebook. In each example, ask several students what they are comparing and if the sentence uses like or as. Have selected students come to the front and underline those words.

Guided Practice: Ask students to find 3 items and write a simile to describe it. Go around the room and ensure that students understand. Help students who are having trouble with this exercise. After students have written their similes, let them share them with the class.

Independent Practice: Hand out the following poems to the class and ask students to highlight the similes in the poem. Students are able to find the similes with the clue words like and as. Students should underline the part of the sentence that compares the object. Correct orally with the class.

Ghosts
Ghosts are scary as a haunted house.
Haunted houses are scary as demons.
Oatmeal is scary as ghouls.
Slimy phantoms are scary as purple knights.
Tea is scary as a Harry Frankenstein.

The Moon and the Sun
The moon is like a sun.
The sun is like a moon.
The sun is like a star.
The star is like a moon.
The star is like a planet.
The planet is like you.
Sweet as you can be.
After you eat a lovely sweet!

Friends
Friends are like family.
They don't get mad if you use a little title for a poem that they made up.
A good friend can't get as mad as a parent can.
Friends are also like a cat, a dog, or a pet.
They are faithful.

Standard: The student will use supporting ideas, details, and facts from a variety of sources to develop and elaborate the topic.

Objective: The student will incorporate vivid language into writing by using similes and details.

Night Writes: Ask 3 students to share their Night Writes™ journal entry with the class. Post "Night Writes™" topic for homework.

Word of the Day: Have students find the "Word of the Day" in the dictionary, copy the definition, and write a complete sentence using the word. Ask several students to read their sentences.

Review: "S" stands for simile. Have students check their definition and examples in the Writer's Notebook. Ensure that students have their samples of similes by asking students to orally read what they have written in their Writer's Notebook under "Notes". Give students the following worksheet to complete the sentences using a simile. Reiterate that similes help create pictures in the mind. Complete the first sentence together. Have students share their answers. Upon completion, write the responses on the board.

Skill Introduction: Students will learn to add more detail to their writing.

Modeling: Explain to students that you are going to give them tips on how make their writing so much clearer and add some excitement. Write the following sentences on the board:

1. An animal went into a building.

2. A dog walked into a house.

3. A Great Dane limped into the doctor's office.

Explain that the first sentence was telling, not showing. When you wrote the second sentence, it was becoming much clearer. As you became even more detailed in sentence three, the writing was showing, not telling. This is key to detailed writing. Students are learning how to "Move down the ladder."

Structured Practice:

1. *Write : **The cat ran.***

2. *Have students circle the noun and underline the verb. Ask specific students which word is the noun and which word is the verb.*

3. *Have students change the verb to make it become more vivid. Call on several students on their choice of verbs.*

4. *Have students give a choice of 1 adverb (how, when or where the action takes place).*

5. *Have students give suggestion on how to add more detail to the end of the sentence.*

6. *Have students suggest types of adjectives to describe any nouns that you could include in the detail.*

7. *Read the sentence to the class.*

8. *Repeat this exercise until the majority of students are able to follow the process. here are suggestions for other sentences: The man walked. The cow ate grass.*

Guided Practice: Write the following sentence on the overhead: *The car moved.* Have students work on moving down the ladder. Write the steps on the overhead. Have students check off each step as they move down the ladder. Go one step at a time. Go around the room and help as needed. Upon completion of the five steps to clearer, more detailed writing, have students share their sentences with the rest of the class. Repeat the process with the next sentence: *The child looked.*

DAY 33
SIMILE WORKSHEET

Similes
A phrase that compares two unlike things in order to describe on of them, using the word like or as.

1. hungry as a _____

2. waddled like a _____

3. worked like _____

4. happy as _____

5. quiet as _____

6. rough as _____

7. heavy as _____

8. walked like _____

9. cheeks like _____

10. deep as _____

11. blind as a _____

12. brave as a _____

13. playful as a _____

14. pretty as a _____

15. sick as _____

16. neat as _____

17. warm as _____

18. hard as _____

19. sly as _____

20. white as _____

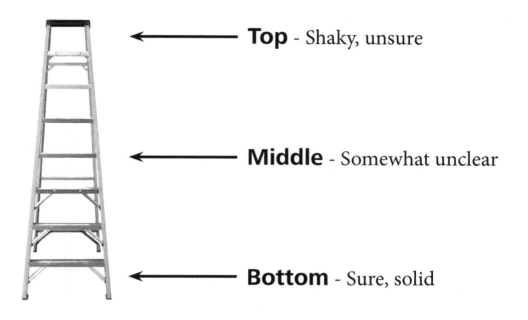

Top - Shaky, unsure

Middle - Somewhat unclear

Bottom - Sure, solid

Five Steps for Moving Down the Ladder

1. Circle the noun and underline the verb.

2. List 2 adjectives (describing words) for the noun.

3. Change the verb to become more vivid.

4. List one adverb (how, when or where the action takes place) for the verb.

5. Add detail to the end of the sentence.

Sample Exercise

Top ⟶ The cat ran.

The furry black cat ran.
The furry black cat scurried.

Middle ⟶ The furry black cat scurried under the desk.

The furry black cat scurried under the desk when the teacher entered the room.

Bottom ⟶ The furry black cat scurried under the dark brown wooden desk when the teacher entered the classroom.

Standard: The student will use supporting ideas, details, and facts from a variety of sources to develop and elaborate the topic.

Objective: The student will incorporate vibrant language into writing by using details.

Night Writes: Ask 3 students to share their Night Writes™ journal entry with the class. Post "Night Writes™" topic for homework.

Word of the Day: Have students find the "Word of the Day" in the dictionary, copy the definition, and write a complete sentence using the word. Ask several students to read their sentences.

Review: Review the steps in moving down the ladder. Ensure that students have copied the 5 steps in their "Notes" section of their "Writer's Notebook". Write the sentence: *The baby cried.* Write the steps on the board. Have students check off each step as they move down the ladder. Go one step at a time. Circulate the classroom and help students as needed. Upon completion of the five steps to clearer, more detailed writing, have students share their sentences with the rest of the class.

Skill Introduction. Students will read examples of effective words and use them in writing. Students will also learn to add more detail to their writing.

Modeling. Explain that you have just received $100 to buy a bicycle. You look on the internet and find the following two advertisements (See attached). Examine Ad # 1 and Ad #2. You decide to buy the bicycle in Ad #2. Demonstrate to students the power of words by writing all of the words in the second advertisement that convinced you to purchase that particular bicycle.

Structured Practice. Show an empty potato chip package to the class. Have students volunteer descriptive advertising words for the product. Record the words on board.

Guided Practice. Place students in groups of four. Hand out an assortment of food products to describe. Have students list at least 15 powerful adjectives that describe these products. Suggestions for food products could range from snacks, candy bars, canned vegetables, fresh fruit, various flavors of soda, and fast food items such as hamburgers, chicken nuggets, and french fries. Go around the room to ensure that students understand the task at hand. Each student needs to be participating in this group assignment and is responsible for copying down the descriptive words. When the list is complete, have one representative from each group share their list with the rest of the class.

Independent Practice. Using their 15 powerful words that describe their food product, have students return to their desks and independently write an appealing advertisement for the food product. Upon completion, allow students time to share their advertisement with their classmates.

AD #1

> Bike for sale – call anytime!
>
> 555-1234

AD #2

> Fabulous bike for sale – perfect condition.
>
> Painted candy apple red with lots of chrome.
>
> Brand new knobby tires – Free bike lock included.
>
> Only $99!!!!! Please call 555-1234 for more details.

DAY 35

Standard: The student will use supporting ideas, details, and facts from a variety of sources to develop and elaborate the topic.

Objective: The student will incorporate vivid language into writing by using color words.

Night Writes: Ask 3 students to share their Night Writes™ journal entry with the class. Post "Night Writes™" topic for homework.

Word of the Day: Have students find the "Word of the Day" in the dictionary, copy the definition, and write a complete sentence using the word. Ask several students to read their sentences.

Review: Review the steps in moving down the ladder. Write the sentence: *The girl talked.* Write the steps on the board. Have students check off each step as they move down the ladder. Go one step at a time. Go around the room and help as needed. Upon completion of the five steps to clearer, more detailed writing, have students share their sentences with the rest of the class.

Skill Introduction. Students will take the eight standard colors and write more specific words. In this manner, students are learning how to add more detail to their writing.

Modeling. Write the eight standard colors on the board. Write one example for each of the eight standard colors that make the color more vivid. See attached sheet for color words.

Structured Practice. Show the color, picture, and your word choice for each word. Have students volunteer another descriptive word for each of the colors. Record the words on chart paper.

Guided Practice. Have students take out their Writer's Notebook and turn to the section labeled "Notes". Have them write color words at the top of the page. Next, have them write each of the eight words (Red, Yellow, Orange, Green, Blue, Purple, Brown, and Black) on a separate sheet of paper. Allow time for students to write a list of words for each color. Circulate the classroom and share some of the words that are exceptional. Comment that students are free to add these words to their list. Remind students that the notebook is to be used as a reference and words and ideas may be added at any time.

Independent Practice. Using their own choices for various color words, have students write a paragraph describing what objects, materials, furniture, etc. can be found in this particular classroom. Upon completion, allow students time to share their classroom description with their classmates.

Final Review: Place the progress chart on the board. Explain that the second writing test will be given tomorrow. Based on the Writing Rubric, students will predict a realistic goal for their second official graded test. Make sure that the rubric is posted in the room as well. In that manner, students can understand how you graded their essay. As a teacher, you may say that after 6 weeks of instruction, you can make another 4 and list what comprises a 4. Then color the second bar up to the number 4 on the chart.

TEST TOMORROW!

Red
Cherry
Fire engine
Brick
Lobster

Orange
Tiger
Pumpkin
Duck feet
Carrot

Yellow
Banana
Buttery
Mustard
School bus

Blue
Sapphire
Ocean
Sky
Turquoise

Green
Emerald
Chalkboard
Shamrock
Olive

Purple
Plum
Periwinkle
Lilac
Lavender

Brown
Chestnut
Cinnamon
Clay
Coffee

Black
Raven
Licorice
Midnight
Jet

DAY 36

Standard: The student will write an expository essay appropriate to the topic, audience and purpose.

Objective: The student will learn how to write their third expository essay independently.

Night Writes: Ask 3 students to share their Night Writes™ journal entry with the class. Post "Night Writes™" topic for homework.

Word of the Day: Have students find the "Word of the Day" in the dictionary, copy the definition, and write a complete sentence using the word. Ask several students to read their sentences.

Review: The graphic organizer and its three components: circle the topic, draw a rectangle around the clue word(s), and underline what the student is to write about. Use examples for review. Review the five parts of the expository essay. Review sample of the introduction (first paragraph), three main ideas (reasons) with details (second, third and fourth paragraphs) and the closing (fifth paragraph). At this point, share selected pieces of student writing that demonstrates excellence from the completion of past topic, Why making good grades is important. Students love praise!

Independent Practice: Explain to students that this is their second official test. Students will be given 45 minutes to plan a graphic organizer (G.O.) and write a 5 paragraph essay on the topic below. Remind students of the goals they set yesterday. Review the scoring and ensure that the writing rubric is posted in the room.

Many students have plans for their future as an adult.

Before you begin writing, think about the career or job in which you might be interested.

Now write to explain how you can best prepare yourself for this career beginning now and continuing into your future.

Standard: The student will use supporting ideas, details, and facts from a variety of sources to develop and elaborate about the topic.

Objective: The student will incorporate vibrant language into writing by using alliteration; utilize elements of style, including word choice and sentence variation; and incorporate adjectives and adverbs.

Night Writes: Ask 3 students to share their Night Writes™ journal entry with the class. Post "Night Writes™" topic for homework.

Word of the Day: Have students find the "Word of the Day" in the dictionary, copy the definition, and write a complete sentence using the word. Ask several students to read their sentences.

Review: "C" stands for color words. Remind students to include several colorful words in each piece of their expository writing. Review the steps in moving down the ladder. Write the sentence: *The boy ran.* Write the steps on the overhead. Have students check off each step as they move down the ladder. Go one step at a time. Circulate throughout the classroom and help as needed. Upon completion of the five steps to clearer, more detailed writing, have students share their sentences.

Skill Introduction: Students will learn to incorporate the use of alliteration, repeating the same letter sound at the beginning of two or more words in a sentence. In this manner, students are learning how to add more detail to their writing.

Modeling: Tell the class you are going to read the following poem that uses a certain style of writing called alliteration.

Laughing Lions and Jumping Jaguars

Laughing lions lovingly laugh like jumping joking jaguars

on top of tall talking trees.

When the towering talking trees start

talking and tattling, the jumping jaguars topple off.

Structured Practice. After reading the poem, explain to the class they are going to write a sentence with alliteration as a group. Write the word "cat" on the overhead and ask students to think of an adjective (a describing word) that begins with the "k" sound. (cool, crazy, cosmic). Then ask them to think of an adjective that begins with the "k" sound. What does the cat do? (climb, crawl, cuddle). Now how did the cat do it? Think of an adverb (describes the action) with the letter sound "k". (cautiously, completely, carefully). Where did the cat do it and what did he catch? Continue until the sentence is written on the overhead. Pick another subject and write another sentence together.

Guided Practice. Have student write five sentences on their own. Circulate throughout the classroom and check for understanding. Compliment those students who really demonstrate excellent sentence writing using alliteration. Have students share their sentences with the class.

Independent Practice. Explain to the class that they are going to write a book using all of the letters of the alphabet. Give each student a blank sheet of white paper. Assign each student a letter from the alphabet and have them write a sentence using that letter and draw a picture portraying that sentence. Tell the students that the book will be compiled in alphabetical order and will be shared with a primary classroom.

Alliterations!! Alliterations!! Alliterations!!

Captivating! Cool! Crazy! Cantankerous! Cats!

Gorgeous! Great! Gregarious! Gruesome! Gorillas!

Standard: The student will use supporting ideas, details, and facts from a variety of sources to develop and elaborate the topic.

Objective: The student will write naturally about their own real life moments in an expository essay.

Night Writes: Ask 3 students to share their Night Writes™ journal entry with the class. Post "Night Writes™" topic for homework.

Word of the Day: Have students find the "Word of the Day" in the dictionary, copy the definition, and write a complete sentence using the word. Ask several students to read their sentences.

Review: "A" stands for alliteration. Remind students to include one piece of alliteration in their expository essay. Review the steps in moving down the ladder. Write the sentence: *The lion roared.* Upon completion of the five steps to clearer, more detailed writing, have students share their sentences.

Skill Introduction: Students will learn to incorporate the use of real life experiences, adding more sizzle to their writing.

Modeling: Explain to students that significant life moments happen every day. Provide an example of a significant life moment that happened to you on your first day as a teacher (See attached sample).

Structured Practice: Talk to the students about their very first day of kindergarten. What do they recall about that day? Explain that the class is going to generate a list of 20 questions that should help them recall the event. Have students close their eyes and think back to their very first day of school. Record the questions on the overhead or chart paper. If a student can't recall all the details, explain that it is perfectly fine to make up an answer. To get the process started, you may wish to lead it by posing one or two questions. Some suggested questions are: What was the weather like that day? What were you wearing? How did you get to school?

Guided Practice: After all 20 questions are recorded on the board, have students copy the questions and record their answers under each question on a separate piece of paper. Circulate throughout the classroom and help students who are having difficulty answering a particular question. Assure students that there is no right or wrong answers. These thoughts are their own personal experiences. Students love to write about their first day of kindergarten when they have enough details to make it interesting. Allow time for students to share some of their experiences with the class.

Independent Practice: Have students pull out their Writer's Notebook and turn to the section titled "Practice Work" and write at least one paragraph (6 to 8 sentences) about their first day of school. Make sure that students outline a graphic organizer before they begin writing their essay. Some of the better writers will be able to write a complete essay about their first day of school.

My First Real Moments as a Writing Teacher

As most teachers know, a lot of hiring of teaching staff takes place at the very last minute. I was no exception. The last week of July, I was getting nervous as I hadn't received any phone calls for interviews. Finally, I answered a phone call for an interview with a principal at an elementary school. With apprehension, I went in for the interview. I was upfront about not having any teaching experience, but also made sure to mention that I was a parent to two children and three stepchildren. After the interview was over, I had no idea of whether or not I would be hired.

On Wednesday afternoon, I received the phone call offering me a position as a writing teacher at the elementary school. I was to start teaching Monday. I had three days to think about whether or not I had made the worst decision of my life.

Monday came. I think I maybe slept for two hours that night as I was a bundle of nerves. I arrived at my new school about an hour early, got the key to my room, and headed down to the classroom.

When I arrived at the classroom, I detected that I had a whiteboard, so I walked over to it to write my name. That's when I discovered that I had nothing to write with. I also did not have a teacher's desk, nothing on the walls, and obviously, no teaching experience. It was up to me to make sure that the students didn't catch on to the fact that I was new to the profession.

The first bell rang and I walked to the door. My day had begun. My impression of the first batch of students was good. The only bad note was during the last class of the day when I heard another student threaten one of his classmates. As I said before, my room had nothing in it, so the only thing I could do was to write the offending student a pass with an explanation of the incident and sent him on his way to the office. About 15 minutes later, he comes back holding a piece of paper. My assistant principal had underlined the proper procedures for sending a student up on a referral. I couldn't believe it. It would have been one thing for her to have pulled me aside, but to hand it to the student who was in trouble did not feel right.

After the students left, I remember thinking to myself how hard I had worked. I also remember thinking that I had finally found my path in life. I have never looked back. Teaching was what I was meant to do.

Standard: The student will use supporting ideas, details, and facts from a variety of sources to develop and elaborate the topic.

Objective: The student will write naturally about their own real life moments in an expository essay.

Night Writes: Ask 3 students to share their Night Writes™ journal entry with the class. Post "Night Writes™" topic for homework.

Word of the Day: Have students find the "Word of the Day" in the dictionary, copy the definition, and write a complete sentence using the word. Ask several students to read their sentences.

Review: Review the steps in moving down the ladder. Write the sentence: *The baby crawled.* Upon completion of the five steps to clearer, more detailed writing, have students share their sentences.

Skill Introduction: Students will learn to incorporate the use of real life experiences, adding more sizzle to their writing.

Modeling: Explain to students that significant life moments happen every day. Provide another example of a significant life moment that happened to you. A series of "firsts" or "bests" are easy ways to come up with topics for writing about these personal experiences. Discuss in detail about how significant life moments are with you every day.

Structured Practice: Talk to the students about their very best friend and how they met. What do they recall about that day? Explain that the class is going to generate a list of 20 questions that should help them recall the event. Have students close their eyes and think back to how they met their best friend. Record the questions on the board. To get the process started, you may wish to lead it by posing one or two questions. Some suggested questions are: Where were you when you first met this person? What did the person look like? What was he or she doing?

Guided Practice: After all 20 questions are recorded on the board, have students copy the questions and record their answers under each question on a separate piece of paper. Circulate throughout the classroom and help students who are having difficulty answering a particular question. Assure students that there is no right or wrong answers. These thoughts are their own personal experiences. Students love to write about how they met their best friend and all the events that happened that day. Make sure students use enough details to make it interesting. Explain to students that they must show, not tell about the event. It's important that students understand their lives do matter. As you circulate throughout the classroom, remind students that these types of stories happen all day long, if we just take notice. Allow time for students to share some of their experiences with the class.

Independent Practice: Have students pull out their Writer's Notebook and turn to the section titled "Practice Work" and write at least two paragraphs (6 to 8 sentences each) about meeting their very best friend. Remind students to prepare a graphic organizer before beginning to write their essay. Some of your better writers will be able to write a complete essay about this event.

Standard: The student will use supporting ideas, details, and facts from a variety of sources to develop and elaborate the topic.

Objective: The student will use the helping words to write naturally about their own real life moments in an expository essay.

Night Writes: Ask 3 students to share their Night Writes™ journal entry with the class. Post "Night Writes™" topic for homework.

Word of the Day: Have students find the "Word of the Day" in the dictionary, copy the definition, and write a complete sentence using the word. Ask several students to read their sentences.

Skill Introduction: Students will learn and apply the "helping words" (the 5 W's and H) in their real life experiences, adding more sizzle to their writing.

Modeling: Introduce the lesson by explaining to students that you wrote a real life experience about your summer vacation and would like to share with the class. Place the following passage on the board and read:

Last summer we went on a trip to Myrtle Beach. We lived in a beach house by the ocean. We did a lot of swimming and played horseshoes on the beach. One day I saw a dolphin. We stayed for only five days. I wish we could go back again this summer.

After reading the above example, think aloud. Say that after reading this experience about your summer vacation that you feel it is missing a lot of detail. It doesn't have any excitement. Tell them that you have learned a great technique that will help make the writing more interesting. Write the 5 W's and H on chart paper. (Who, What, Where, When, Why and How).

Structured Practice: Ask students if they would like to know more about your trip. If you gave them more details, could they picture it better? Explain that more details help readers to "see" it better by using details. For instance, **who** are the other people I call 'we?" Are they relatives? **What** are their names? Discuss that these "helping words", make it easier to include a lot more details. Point to the helping words and ask the class if they can think of more questions to ask. (Suggestions: **Why** did you stay only five days? **Where** is Myrtle Beach? **How** far is it from your home? **Why** did you pick Myrtle Beach? **When** did you see the dolphin? **What** color was the dolphin? How big was the dolphin? Could you see it jump in the water? **What** did the beach house look like?)

Structured Practice: Have students pull out their Writer's Notebook and turn to the section titled "Notes". Have students write "Helping Words" and the 5 W's and H in their notebook. Explain to students that these are words newspaper reporters use over and over again to help write their newspaper articles. Place an article on the board. Point out the headline. Ask the student what the headline does? Does it capture their attention? Does it answer any of the 5Ws and H? Read through the article a paragraph at a time until all of the 5Ws and 1H questions are answered. Write "Who, What, When, Where, Why and How" on the overhead. Beside each, have students write the answer to the question from your sample clipping and where in the news article they found the answer (headline, paragraph 1, paragraph 2, etc.)

Independent Practice: Have students turn to the section titled "Practice Work" in their Writer's Notebook and write at least three paragraphs (6 to 8 sentences each) about a summer vacation or memorable trip. Remind students to use a graphic organizer and their "helping words".

Final Review: Place the progress chart on the board. Explain that the third writing test will be given tomorrow. Based on the Writing Rubric, students will predict a realistic goal for their third official graded test. Make sure that the rubric is posted in the room as well. In that manner, students can understand how they predicted their score. As a teacher, you may say that after 7 weeks of instruction, you can make at least another 4 and then list what comprises a 4. Then have students color the third bar up to the number 4 or higher on the chart.

TEST TOMORROW!

Who? _____

What? _____

When? _____

Where? _____

Why? _____

How? _____

DAY 41

Standard: The student will write an expository essay appropriate to the topic, audience and purpose.

Objective: The student will learn how to write their third expository essay independently.

Night Writes: Ask 3 students to share their Night Writes™ journal entry with the class. Post "Night Writes™" topic for homework.

Word of the Day: Have students find the "Word of the Day" in the dictionary, copy the definition, and write a complete sentence using the word. Ask several students to read their sentences.

Review: The graphic organizer and its three components: circle the topic, draw a rectangle around the clue word(s), and underline what the student is to write about. Use examples for review. Review the five parts of the expository essay. Review sample of introductions (first paragraph), three main ideas (reasons) with details (second, third and fourth paragraphs) and the closing (fifth paragraph). At this point, share selected pieces of student writing that demonstrates excellence from the completion of last week's topic, "How you can prepare yourself for a career or job that you might be interested." Students love praise!

Independent Practice: Explain to students that this is their third official test. Students will be given 45 minutes to plan a graphic organizer (G.O.) and write a 5 paragraph essay on the topic below. Remind students of the goals they set yesterday. Review the scoring and ensure that the writing rubric is posted in the room.

Everyone has a special activity they like to do outside.

Before you begin writing, think about the special activity you like to do outside.

Now write to explain what makes your activity fun.

Standard: The student will use supporting ideas, details, and facts from a variety of sources to develop and elaborate about the topic.

Objective: The student will develop the topic with supporting details and precise verbs.

Night Writes: Ask 3 students to share their Night Writes™ journal entry with the class. Post "Night Writes™" topic for homework.

Word of the Day: Have students find the "Word of the Day" in the dictionary, copy the definition, and write a complete sentence using the word. Ask several students to read their sentences.

Review: "R" stands for real life moments. Remind students that in each piece of expository writing, they should include a minimum of one real life moment or personal experience in their writing.

Skill Introduction: Students will learn how to enhance their writing by replacing old, over-used plain verbs with exciting verbs that stimulate reader interest.

Modeling: Explain that verbs are the words in a sentence that show the movement, the actions, or the process taking place in the sentence. Good verb choice engages the reader. Write the following sentence on the board: *The man **walked** across the road.* Tell students you are going to replace the underlined verb with a more exciting verb: *The man **staggered** across the road.* The underlined verb is a much more exciting verb. Write : *The man **stumbled** across the road.* Explain that there are many other exciting verbs other than using walk as a verb. Write: *The man **darted** across the road.* Tell students that there are even more choices than walk.

Structured Practice: Place the word "walked" on the board. Include the previous verbs (staggered, stumbled, darted) on the list. Ask students what other action or vivid verbs could be used in place of walk. Upon completion of the verb walk, write the following sentence: *A snake **comes** towards me.* Ask students to name verbs that are much more exciting than the verb "coming". As a class, compose a list of vivid verbs. Write: *The child **asks** for a snack.* Repeat the same procedure as demonstrated in the previous two exercises. See attached list for suggestions,

Guided Practice: Place the following verbs on the board. In their Writer's Notebook, under the section titled, "Notes," have students think of as many synonyms for each of these 6 boring verbs:

jump like talk ran walk went

Circulate throughout the classroom to ensure that students understand the assignment. Upon completion, pick students who have an abundance of verbs to share with the class. Inform students that they may wish to add these verbs to their list as well.

Independent Practice: In their Writer's Notebook under the section titled, "Practice Work", have students write at least one page about a special place they would like to go. Explain that the real life moment is based on a personal experience. Because many students have such limited background knowledge, explain that the place could be anything from spending time with a friend or relative, playing at the park, riding a bike, etc. In their writing piece, have the student explain why they like going to that special place and use at least six vivid verbs from their compiled list. Remind students to plan a graphic organizer before beginning this written assignment.

The man **walked** across the road.

    The man **staggered** across the road.

    The man **stumbled** across the road.

    The man **darted** across the road.

    The man **sauntered** across the road.

    The man **strolled** across the road.

    The man **marched** across the road.

    The man **ambled** across the road.

The child **asks** for a snack.

    The child **demands** a snack.

    The child **whines** for a snack.

    The child **begs** for a snack.

    The child **screams** for a snack.

    The child **whimpers** for a snack.

    The child **pleads** for a snack.

A snake is **coming** towards me.

    A snake is **slithering** towards me.

    A snake is **approaching** towards me.

    A snake is **sneaking** towards me.

    A snake is **gliding** towards me.

    A snake is **slinking** towards me.

    A snake is **drawing closer** towards me.

    A snake is **stretching closer** towards me.

Standard: The student will use supporting ideas, details, and facts from a variety of sources to develop and elaborate the topic.

Objective: The student will develop the topic with supporting details by using action and descriptive words.

Night Writes: Ask 3 students to share their Night Writes™ journal entry with the class. Post "Night Writes™" topic for homework.

Word of the Day: Have students find the "Word of the Day" in the dictionary, copy the definition, and write a complete sentence using the word. Ask several students to read their sentences.

Review: "V" stands for vivid verbs. Remind students that in each piece of expository writing, they should include vivid verbs. Have students add the **verb tell**. Ask for volunteers who can give a more vivid verb for tell (inform, advise, notify, report, declare, expose, and reveal and just a few suggestions).

Skill Introduction: Students will use action and descriptive words to show a character's emotions, feelings, and internal responses to events.

Modeling: Emphasize the idea that words can be used to capture strong emotions. Explain that good writers let the reader know what characters are thinking about when something happens. It is not enough to just tell what a character is feeling. Good writers show what a character is feeling.

Structured Practice: Ask students to help create a list of emotions that the characters in their stories might have. Record emotions on the overhead or whiteboard. Tell students that one way to make emotions more powerful is to stretch out the moment by recording the character's actions, facial expressions, gestures, and movements. Read the following example aloud:

Johnny was really mad!

> *vs.*

Johnny's hands coiled into two firm fists. His face turned scarlet red as he glared at his big brother. Unexpectedly Johnny flung his baseball glove across the living room. He whipped around and stomped up the stairs. His bedroom door banged shut, reverberating throughout the whole house.

Discuss what makes the second paragraph a more powerful example. The second example is a better way to include emotions because it **shows** Johnny's actions, facial expressions, and body language. Ask for volunteers to choose an emotion and act out the emotion (see attached). Think about face, body, and movement. Have the rest of the class guess the emotion. Share how they could write what they saw and heard. Model those words and examples on the board by writing a description of the setting.

DAY 43
USING EMOTIONS

Guided Practice: Assign an emotion to each student. Tell students that they are not to reveal the emotion to classmates. They will need to portray the assigned emotion through writing. In their Writer's Notebook under the section titled "Practice Work", have students write their own paragraph to reveal the emotion they have been assigned. Upon completion, have students read their paragraph and have classmates guess the emotion through their writing. Circulate throughout the classroom and assist students who need additional help with this assignment.

Independent Practice: In yesterday's assignment, "A Special Place I Like to Go", students were asked to incorporate the use of vivid verbs. For today's independent practice, have students reread their written work and find places where they can add more emotion by inserting more actions, facial expressions, and body language to reveal a certain attitude or mood.

excited	nervous	sad
joyful	confused	bored
jealous	embarassed	hungry
tired	amazed	horrified
guilty	greedy	cheerful
impatient	angry	shy
scared	worried	surprised
lonely	shocked	exhausted
panicked	disappointed	anxious

Standard: The student will use supporting ideas, details, and facts from a variety of sources to develop and elaborate about the topic.

Objective: The student will develop the topic with supporting details and precise verbs.

Night Writes: Ask 3 students to share their Night Writes™ journal entry with the class. Post "Night Writes™" topic for homework.

Word of the Day: Have students find the "Word of the Day" in the dictionary, copy the definition, and write a complete sentence using the word. Ask several students to read their sentences.

Review: "E" stands for emotions. Remind students that in each piece of expository writing, they should include emotions. Demonstrate how it is done by taking one emotion yourself. Look at your emotion without showing it to the class. Write a short paragraph in front of the class. (You may wish to pick an emotion ahead of time so you can preplan your writing). Think aloud as you complete this writing process. It is now time for students to demonstrate their ability to write about emotions. Assign each of the students a different emotion from yesterday. Tell students that their word may not be used in the paragraph. Students must reveal the emotion only though the words, thoughts or actions of the characters in their paragraph. Remind students that one way to make emotions more powerful is to stretch out the moment by recording the character's actions, facial expressions, gestures, and movements.

Skill Introduction: Students will learn how to create vivid imagery by incorporating onomatopoeia in their expository writing. Onomatopoeias are words that illustrate sound such as bang, boom, click, swish, clap, creak and beep. They can be used to help writing come to life for the reader.

Modeling: Think aloud! Make various sounds and then explain what sound you are making. For instance, you might say, Peep! Peep! – that's the sound a baby chick makes. Woof! Woof! That's the sound a dog can make." Other suggestions: Boom! Boom! (big bass drum), Rrrrip! (a rag tearing).

Structured Practice: Write the following words on the overhead. Ask students to single out animals and objects that might be associated with these sounds.

beep	splash	clap	fizz	sizzle	roar
snap	hiss	quack	chirp	zoom	whack
munch	boom	rattle	splash	bang	gurgle

Guided Practice: Provide each student with a sound chart (See page 112). The sound chart has three columns. The students listen to everyday sounds (on tape or in person) and write what is making the sound in the first column. On the second column the students write the onomatopoeia that describes the sound and then use the sound word in a sentence in the third column. After furnishing the sound, circulate throughout the classroom to ensure that students understand how to write and identify onomatopoeia.

Independent Practice: Students will use their sound charts to create their own story. While the students are creating their own sound page the teacher will circulate throughout the group to assess understanding of the lesson and provide further instruction if necessary.

DAY 44
SOUNDS

Sound Word Chart

Sound	Onomatopoeia	Sentence
air	whoosh	*Mary whooshes past with no feet on the pedals, then no hands.*

Standard: The student will use supporting ideas, details, and facts from a variety of sources to develop and elaborate the topic.

Objective: The student will develop the topic with supporting details and precise verbs.

Night Writes: Ask 3 students to share their Night Writes™ journal entry with the class. Post "Night Writes™" topic for homework.

Word of the Day: Have students find the "Word of the Day" in the dictionary, copy the definition, and write a complete sentence using the word. Ask several students to read their sentences.

Review: "S" stands for sounds. Remind students that in each piece of expository writing, students should include a bit of onomatopoeia (sound words). Onomatopoeias are words that illustrate sound such as bang, boom, click, whoosh, bang creak and beep. They can be used to help writing come to life for the reader. Ask students to describe these sounds: A balloon being burst. Someone eating crispy cheese snacks. A tiny bell being rung.

Skill Introduction: Students will learn to use the acronym, "SCARVES" to enhance and add more sizzle to their writing.

Modeling: Place the acronym "SCARVES" on the overhead. Explain to students they now know all of the additional tricks to make their writing more exciting and interesting. Tell them that this is going to be their helping word that will be placed on their graphic organizer which will serve as a reminder to make sure they use at least one of these elements in each piece of expository writing. Review what each of the letter stands for: **S** means similes, **C** means color words, **A** means alliteration, **R** means real life moments, **V** means vivid verbs, **E** means emotions, and **S** means sounds.

SCARVES

S - Similes
C - Color Words
A - Alliteration
R - Real Life Moments
V - Vivid Verbs
E - Emotions
S - Sounds

DAY 45
SCARVES

Structured Practice: Call out each letter on the "SCARVES" chart and ask students to provide an example. Practice this exercise until every student has had an opportunity to participate. Have students elaborate on their examples. For example, when a student states that "R" means Real Life Moment, have the student share a real life moment with the class. Let the student provide as much detail as possible. When students provide an example of a vivid verbs, ask why this is a better choice. After all students have participated, cover up the "SCARVES" chart and ask students what each of the letters stand for. Ensure that all students have had a chance to answer.

Guided Practice: Have students pull out their Writer's Notebook and turn to the section titled "Notes." Place the "SCARVES" chart on the overhead. And have students copy the "SCARVES" chart. Next, have students think of a time of when they were embarrassed. With that in mind, have students write a paragraph about that real life moment by incorporating emotions, similes, color words, alliteration, and sounds. Encourage the more proficient writing students to write more than a paragraph. Circulate throughout the classroom to ensure students understand the assignment and help those who need it. Allow time for students to share their experiences.

Final Review: Place the progress chart on the overhead. Explain that the fourth writing test will be given tomorrow. Based on the Writing Rubric, students will predict a realistic goal for their fourth official graded test. Make sure that the rubric is posted in the room as well. In that manner, students can understand how they predicted their score. As a teacher, you may say that after 8 weeks of instruction, students should be setting their standards a bit higher. For example, if a student scored a 3 on the last test, a 4 would be a reasonable goal. If a student scored a 4 on the last test, the student may feel comfortable to set a goal to score a 5 on this upcoming test. Then have students color the fourth bar up to their predicted number on their chart.

TEST TOMORROW!

Standard: The student will write an expository essay appropriate to the topic, audience and purpose.

Objective: The student will write their fourth expository essay independently.

Night Writes: Ask 3 students to share their Night Writes™ journal entry with the class. Post "Night Writes™" topic for homework.

Word of the Day: Have students find the "Word of the Day" in the dictionary, copy the definition, and write a complete sentence using the word. Ask several students to read their sentences.

Review: The graphic organizer and its three components: circle the topic, draw a rectangle around the clue word(s), and underline what the student is to write about. Use examples for review. Review the five parts of the expository essay. Review samples of introductions (first paragraph), three main ideas (reasons) with details (second, third and fourth paragraphs) and the closing (fifth paragraph). Remind students to write SCARVES and their "helping words" along the side of their graphic organizer. See attached sample of graphic organizer format using SCARVES and helping words.

Independent Practice: Explain to students that this is their fourth official test. Students will be given 45 minutes to plan a graphic organizer (G.O.) and write a 5 paragraph essay on the topic below. Remind students of the goals they set yesterday. Review the scoring and ensure that the writing rubric is posted in the room.

- *We all have a favorite day of the week.*

- *Think about your favorite day of the week.*

- *Now write to explain to your reader why this day of the week is your favorite one.*

SCARVES

S - Similes
C - Color Words
A - Alliteration
R - Real Life Moments
V - Vivid Verbs
E - Emotions
S - Sounds

Helping Words

Who
What
When
Where
Why
How

Topic

Main Idea

Tell

Explain

Supporting details

Personal experience or story

Main Idea

Tell

Explain

Supporting details

Personal experience or story

Main Idea

Tell

Explain

Supporting details

Personal experience or story

Conclusion

Standard: The student will review and use a classroom rubric for written work and use for peer review and editing.

Objective: The student will review the writing rubric, how an essay is scored, and view various exemplary elements of students' essays from yesterday's expository writing test. Students will also learn how to add more detail by including sensory words in their writing.

Night Writes: Ask 3 students to share their Night Writes™ journal entry with the class. Post "Night Writes™" topic for homework.

Word of the Day: Have students find the "Word of the Day" in the dictionary, copy the definition, and write a complete sentence using the word. Ask several students to read their sentences.

Review: Review the writing rubric and what constitutes a score from 0 to 6. Remind students that good expository writing is full of information, descriptions, reasons, and supporting details. From yesterday's test, pick out various components from student essays that demonstrate exemplary writing.

Teacher Notes: Yes, this task does require additional time but the benefits far outweigh your time involved. Students love to see their work on the overhead. Students love praise. Try to find at least one example of the following so that students understand what represents an excellent paper. Give credit by including the student's name!

Great Grabber	Great Transition Words	Cool Conclusion
Similes	Real Life Moments	Expressing Emotion
Color Words	Alliteration	Vivid Verbs
Sounds	Great Use of Vocabulary	Great Title
Great Detail	Graphic Organizer	Sensory Words

DAY 47

Skill Introduction: Students will learn to add sensory words to their expository writing. Sensory words are words/adjectives pertaining to the five senses---taste, touch, smell, sight, hear.

Modeling: Explain to students that you are going to recall a special occasion that you will never forget. Ask students to close their eyes as your read the following passage:

My thirteenth birthday was the best one I ever had. I had a cake and presents that were placed on the dining room table. I had no idea what was in any of the gift boxes. The cake was pretty and very tasty. I had a wonderful time.

Ask students if they could picture the memory and did they feel they were there. (The answer should be no, as there was not enough detail.)

Structured Practice: Read the attached passage to the students. Ask students if it was effortless this time to imagine being part of the memory. Show the second passage on the overhead and ask students to point out the descriptive words using their senses as a guide for determining them. Underline the adjectives as students call them out. Next, use the Sensory Chart (see attached) and write "Birthday Party" as the topic. Under the five senses, write the descriptive words from the passage that were underlined to complete the chart.

Guided Practice: In their Writer's Notebook under the section titled "Notes", have students write the Sensory Words at the top of the page. Provide students with several adjectives for each sense. Explain to students that they are to write at least ten adjectives under each sensory word. Allow time for students to share some of their sensory words with the rest of the class.

Independent Practice: Have students pick out 3 sensory words from each column and write a descriptive sentence for each of the 15 selected words.

My Thirteenth Birthday Party

I was so surprised the day of my birthday. It just happened to be a crisp, cool, fall Saturday morning. Red cardinals were perched on the window sill seeming to be chirping about this special day.

The dining room was all decorated with white and carnation pink ribbons. Sweet-scented roses in creamy white and pink lined the dining room buffet. There were heart-shaped and rose-covered balloons– thirteen of them floating in the dining room.

The 3-foot long cake was sitting on a flimsy lace tablecloth right in the middle of the dining room table.

There were 13 pink candles in the shape of a heart right in the center of this rectangular cake. Pastel pink roses with green leaves peaked out around each petal - they looked so real. The sugary icing was white. The cake was my favorite flavor – chocolate.

We had creamy chocolate chip ice cream to go with it, the kind with the tiny dark chocolate chunks swirled all throughout. I couldn't wait to taste the cake as I anticipated how moist and sweet it would be.

I just knew I was going to have a fabulous time!

Sensory Word Chart

Taste	Touch	Smell	Sight	Hear

DAY 48

Standard: The student will review and use a classroom rubric for written work and use for review and editing.

Objective: The student will review the writing rubric, how an essay is scored, and reviews their previous expository writing test. Students will continue to learn how to add more detail by including sensory words in their writing.

Night Writes: Ask 3 students to share their Night Writes™ journal entry with the class. Post "Night Writes™" topic for homework.

Word of the Day: Have students find the "Word of the Day" in the dictionary, copy the definition, and write a complete sentence using the word. Ask several students to read their sentences.

Review: Before passing out student tests, again review the scoring rubric and what constitutes a score from 0 to 6. Remind students that good expository writing is full of information, descriptions, reasons, and supporting details. Share student expository essays (5 or higher) that demonstrate excellence on the assigned writing topic, "What is your favorite day of the week and explain why it is your favorite day of the week." ***Students love praise!***

Ensure that students place this fourth expository writing piece in their Writer's Notebook under the section titled, "Writing Tests." Next, have students flip to the Progress Chart located in their Writer's Notebook. Have them draw and color in the bar for their actual fourth test score and compare it to their prediction (goal). Ask students to raise their hand if they met their goal. Circulate throughout the classroom and ask each student for one thing they can do to improve their writing on tomorrow's final writing test. Next, have students draw and color the bar for the prediction (goal) of their final writing test.

Final Review: Explain to students that this is the last day before the fifth and final expository writing test. This day will be spent reviewing all of the components that constitute a great piece of expository writing. Remind students of the steps to take before they begin writing. Below follows a summary of the information that needs to be reviewed with your students.

1. Circle the topic, draw a rectangle around the clue word(s), and underline what you are to write about.

2. Plan to take no more than 10 minutes to complete your graphic organizer. Make sure that you write SCARVES and "Helping Words" in the margin.

3. Plan to write five paragraphs for your expository essay. Allow 30 minutes to complete your essay.

4. Paragraph #1 is your introduction. Begin with a great grabber. Restate the topic and describe it. Give three main ideas or examples. End with a transition that guides you into the next paragraph.

5. Paragraphs #2, 3, and 4 are the body of your essay. Use a transition at the beginning of each paragraph. In each paragraph you expand one of your points as completely as you can, restating the main idea (reason) and then expanding on it with supporting details and real life moments that support it. These are the crucial paragraphs that the judges review in the grading of the State Assessment Test. Remember that each of these paragraphs need an introductory and concluding sentence. These are also the paragraphs that you use your "Words of the Day" to show your knowledge of great vocabulary. It's always fabulous if you can inject a bit of humor and creativity.

6. Paragraph #5 is your conclusion. Begin with a cool conclusion word and restate your topic using different words from the introductory paragraph. Summarize paragraphs 2, 3, and 4. Write a one sentence conclusion and end with something witty that will make your reader think or smile.

In addition to the 6 main points, remind students of the following:

1. Stick to the topic and keep the expository essay organized.

2. Use SCARVES as a reminder to include similes, color words, alliteration, real life moments, vivid verbs, emotions, sounds and sensory words.

3. Write all of the helping words in the margin to stimulate thoughts and ideas that should be included in the essay.

4. Be sure to include 5 words from your Writer's Notebook and make them your own. Include them in every expository essay.

5. Be sure that the topic relates to every paragraph and that supporting sentences directly relate to the main points. Start your sentences differently.

6. Allow time to review the essay for content and format. It is perfectly acceptable to insert additional words and phrases, erase and replace with a more vivid verb, or check for grammatical, punctuation, and spelling errors.

7. To ensure you finish on time, break up each section (10 minutes for planning, 30 minutes for writing, and five minutes for revision).

Independent Practice: Have students complete each of the prompts in five minutes or less. When five minutes has passed, collect the G.O. and move on to the next prompt. This exercise is invaluable as it stimulates thinking and forces students to organize their thoughts.

DAY 48
EXPOSITORY ESSAY REVIEW

1. Circle the topic, draw a rectangle around the clue word(s), and underline what you are to write about.

2. Plan to take no more than 10 minutes to complete your graphic organizer. Make sure that you write SCARVES and "Helping Words" in the margin.

3. Plan to write five paragraphs for your expository essay. Allow 30 minutes to complete your essay.

4. Paragraph #1 is your introduction. Begin with a great grabber. Restate the topic and describe it. Give three main ideas or examples. End with a transition that guides you into the next paragraph.

5. Paragraphs #2, 3, and 4 are the body of your essay. Use a transition at the beginning of each paragraph. In each paragraph you expand one of your points as completely as you can, restating the main idea (reason) and then expanding on it with supporting details and real life moments that support it. These are the crucial paragraphs that the judges review in the grading of the State Assessment Test. Remember that each of these paragraphs need an introductory and concluding sentence. These are also the paragraphs that you use your "Words of the Day" to show your knowledge of great vocabulary. It's always fabulous if you can inject a bit of humor and creativity.

6. Paragraph #5 is your conclusion. Begin with a cool conclusion word and restate your topic using different words from the introductory paragraph. Summarize paragraphs 2, 3, and 4. Write a one sentence conclusion and end with something witty that will make your reader think or smile.

Practice G.O. Prompts

Prompt #1

You are a mailperson. You deliver mail to the most famous people in the world.

Before you begin writing, think about what people live on your mail route.

Now explain what people are on your mail route.

Prompt #2

Everyone has something they like to do.

Before you begin writing, think about something you like to do.

Now explain why you like this activity.

Prompt #3

We all have a favorite subject to learn about.

Before you begin writing, think about one subject that is your favorite to learn about in school.

Now write to explain why that subject is your favorite.

Prompt #4

Suppose you could have any animal in the world for a classroom pet.

Before you begin writing, think about what animal you would like to have for a classroom pet.

Now write to explain why this animal should be your classroom pet.

Standard: The student will write an expository essay appropriate to the topic, audience and purpose.

Objective: The student will write their fifth and final expository essay independently.

Review: The graphic organizer and its three components: circle the topic, draw a rectangle around the clue word(s), and underline what the student is to write about. Use examples for review. Review the five parts of the expository essay. Review samples of introductions (first paragraph), three reasons with details (second, third and fourth paragraphs) and the closing (fifth paragraph). Remind students to write SCARVES and their "helping words" along the side of their graphic organizer. See previous sample of graphic organizer format using SCARVES and helping words (page 116).

Independent Practice: Explain to students that this is their fifth official test. Students will be given 45 minutes to plan a graphic organizer (G.O.) and write a 5 paragraph essay on the topic below. Remind students of the goals they set yesterday. Review the scoring and ensure that the writing rubric is posted in the room.

Everyone has a favorite type of weather.

Before you begin writing, think about your favorite type of weather.

Now explain to the reader of your paper what you enjoy doing in this type of weather.

DAY 50

Standard: The student uses the classroom rubric for peer review and editing.

Objective: The student will learn how to understand the writing rubric and how an essay is scored.

Review: Have students turn to the "Scoring" section of their Writer's Notebook. Review the scoring in detail to ensure that all students understand how their papers will be graded.

Skill Introduction: The student will analyze and score expository essays by using the classroom writing rubric.

Modeling: Walk students through the Graphic Organizer (G.O.) as a structural guide to writing for expository writing. Discuss each of the five paragraphs.

> **Introduction:** Two parts – an interesting grabber to catch the reader's attention (the hook!) and a topic sentence that briefly and clearly states what this piece of writing is going to be about. It also states that three main ideas of the essay.

> **Body:** The body is made up of three paragraphs. Each paragraph contains a main idea that explains what the paragraph is about and includes at least 3 to 4 supporting details per paragraph.

> **Conclusion:** The final paragraph summarizes the three reasons and restates the topic.

Review the posted classroom rubric and how a judge would score an expository essay.
See Day 28 for scoring.

Structured Practice: From yesterday's assignment, pick out various student essays and place on the overhead. Do not disclose the name of the student unless the piece of writing is well done. After reading the essay, point to the rubric and start at the 0 and work your way up to a 6. Based on the rubric, ask students to raise their hands if the essay deserves a score of 0, 1, 2, 3, 4, 5, or 6. Tally the numbers for each score and come to consensus on what the class agrees is acceptable and reasonable. Reiterate what the criteria for each of the scores if there seems to be a discrepancy. Remind students that the essay must include the four components – focus, organization, supporting details, and a limited amount of spelling and grammatical errors.

Teachers Note: Students love to see their work displayed and love the recognition. As this is the last official day of writing instruction for expository writing, ensure that all students receive specific praise. Remember that every student has at least one redeeming quality in their writing that can be recognized. You may however, have to search a bit to find that one element that makes it special.

Students are now ready to take the State Assessment Test. Additional prompts have been included at the end of this book for more practice if needed.

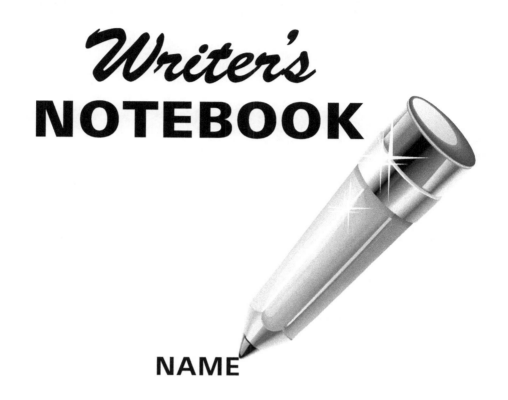

Writer's NOTEBOOK

NAME

_____

TEACHER'S NAME

_____

ALL ABOUT THE WRITER

(Draw Your Picture)

Night Writes™ Topics

1. Tell me about your family.

2. Who is your favorite teacher? Why?

3. Ten things that make you sad.

4. Explain why or why you do not like your name.

5. What do you like and dislike about where you live.

6. Write about the bravest thing you have ever done.

7. If you could be a super hero, what powers would you have?

8. What makes you special or unique?

9. What is your favorite color? Write the reasons for choosing this color.

10. Describe how you look when you make your funniest face.

11. Explain how it feels to be sick.

12. Do you think that you have a lot of self-confidence? Explain the reasons for your answer.

13. What is one goal or hope you have for the future? Explain your answer.

14. How would you feel if there was a new law forbidding the playing of music?

15. Do you think you are shy? What advice could you give to someone who is shy?

16. Who is a hero of yours? Explain why that person means so much to you.

17. Explain why you would or would not like to get married some day.

18. Would you rather be a dog or a cat? Write the reasons for your choice.

19. What is the food you would least like to give up for the rest of your life? Explain why.

20. Would you like to live to be a 100 years old? Explain your answer.

21. If you could be a superstar in any sport when you grow up, what sport would you choose? Explain your answer.

22. What do you like most about yourself? What do you like least about yourself? Explain your answers.

23. What game or toy would you like to have that you don't have? Explain your choice.

24. What do you like most about living in your city? What do you like least about it? Explain your answers.

25. If you could spend an hour with the President of the United States, here are some questions that I would like to ask.

26. What are the things that make you grouchy?

27. Ten things that I want to accomplish by the time I am 40 years old.

28. Someone that I will never forget is _____. Explain why you will never forget this person.

29. A good movie that I have seen is _____. Explain why this is a good movie.

30. America's greatest athlete is _____. Why do you believe this is America's greatest athlete?

31. What are some of the rules you have to follow at home?

32. My list of things that need to be changed at the school.

33. My list of things that I will never do.

34. The best vacation would be . . . .

35. My reasons why everyone should have a pet.

36. A planet that I might like to visit is _____. Why?

37. The best thing that has happened to me recently is _____. Explain why.

38. What would you do if a bully bothered you on your way home?

39. What would happen if you found gold in your backyard?

40. What do you like to do in your free time?

41. If I would get anything in the world for my birthday, it would be _____. I would do what with it.

42. My most favorite holiday is _____. Explain.

43. You have an extra $100 to give away. You cannot spend it on yourself. What would you do with the money?

44. How would you make this world a better place to live in?

45. What would you do if you were Principal for a day?

46. If you could change places with anyone, who would it be and why?

47. Ten crazy reasons why I couldn't do my homework.

48. What is the nicest thing you have done for someone?

49. Tell me about your best friend. Why is that person your best friend?

50. What would happen if children ruled the world?

Word of the Day

1. writer
2. elated
3. deceive
4. absurd
5. vanquish
6. tedious
7. classify
8. casual
9. cantankerous
10. affluent
11. hermit
12. brawl
13. luminous
14. belligerent
15. bedlam
16. dapper
17. curtail
18. dejected
19. remedy
20. germinate
21. digress
22. heirloom
23. foreign
24. docile
25. admonish
26. harass
27. peer
28. stagnant
29. hazardous
30. ventriloquist
31. indulge
32. destitute
33. maneuver
34. frantic
35. unkempt
36. humdrum
37. outwit
38. glamorous
39. diligent
40. efficient
41. betray
42. barricade
43. lecture
44. replenish
45. ingenious
46. knickknack
47. enthusiasm
48. dapper
49. abscond
50. gallery

Prompt #1

Everyone has a favorite color.

Before you begin writing, think about your favorite color and how it makes you feel.

Now explain why it is your favorite color.

Prompt #2

Eating healthy foods is important.

Before you begin writing, think about why it is important to eat healthy foods.

Now explain why you should eat healthy foods.

Prompt #3

People often say one thing but act another way.

Before you begin writing, think about someone who behaves in this manner.

Explain why you think this behavior is not a behavior that you respect.

Prompt #4

Many children have been told some time or another that they were too young or old to do something.

Before you begin writing, think about an activity that you might be too young or old to experience.

Now explain why you think this decision seems unfair.

Prompt #5

Recycling is important to our environment.

Before you begin writing, think about recycling in your community.

Now explain what type of recycling your community does.

Prompt #6

Every school has rules

Before you begin writing, think about your school's rules.

Now explain what rules you would like to change.

Prompt #7

We all have heard that it is important to be a good reader.

Before you begin writing, think about why it is important to be a good reader.

Now explain why you think it is important to be a good reader.

Prompt #8

Everyone enjoys time with their family.

Before you begin writing, think about the best day you ever spent with your family.

Now explain why this is the best day you ever spent with your family.

Prompt #9

Television characters live a life that is too good to be true.

Before you begin writing, think about the television characters that you would like to be.

Now explain what television characters you would like to be.

Prompt #10

School lunches have a bad reputation.

Before you begin writing, think about the lunches you have eaten at school.

Now explain how you could get more students to buy lunch at school.

CPSIA information can be obtained
at www.ICGtesting.com
Printed in the USA
BVHW011454040222
627723BV00004B/28